What Did We Do to **Deserve This?**

What Did We Do to Deserve This?

Palestinian Life under Occupation in the West Bank

Mark Howell

Garnet
PUBLISHING

*With thanks to Boo
for sowing a seed,
Jocelyn for
encouraging its growth
and Morag for
helping it to flower*

What Did We Do To Deserve This?

Published by
Garnet Publishing Limited
8 Southern Court, South Street
Reading RG1 4QS, UK
Tel: +44 (0) 118 959 7847
Fax: +44 (0) 118 959 7356
E-mail: enquiries@garnetpublishing.co.uk
Website: www.garnetpublishing.co.uk

First edition

ISBN 978-1-85964-195-8

British Library Cataloguing-in-Publication Data. A catalogue record
for this book is available from the British Library.

Credits
Editorial: Dan Nunn
Production: Nick Holroyd
Design: David Rose
Maps on page 17 used courtesy of GEOprojects (UK) Ltd.
Maps on pages 31 and 79 used courtesy of OCHA-oPt.
Printed and bound by International Press, Lebanon

Caption to previous page
Boy looking through security gate as his mother
waits for the green light to come on so they can
pass through Qalandia "border" crossing from
the West Bank to East Jerusalem, one integral
territory under international law

Contents

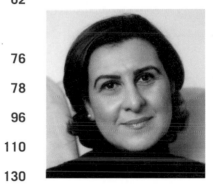

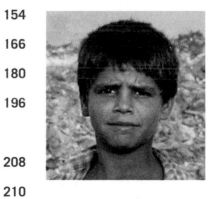

Author's note

This book shows the current reality of Palestinian life, day to day, in the West Bank. It also places it in context by explaining the origins of the Israeli-Palestinian conflict and the motivations behind Israel's current policy. Finally, it looks to the future and assesses what options remain for the Palestinians and where events may lead. The conflict is usually portrayed as complex and insoluble. In reality, Israel's policies in the West Bank have changed very little over the past 40 years and the issues at stake are readily understandable. This book is intended to leave the reader with a rounded understanding of these issues and the reasons why a solution seems so out of reach. Although it is focused very much on what is happening now, the first few chapters are inevitably historically-slanted, setting the context. No prior knowledge of the region is required and the book is designed to be easy to read. There are many important, more academic-orientated books available for those who wish to explore the situation further and I hope for some this work will serve as a stepping stone to them.

The book has evolved from a photographic project which I initiated on my first visit to the West Bank in August 2005. I arrived without any fixed ideas but was keen to see for myself what was happening on the ground, having been acquainted with the situation from a distance, largely through the British media. However, it did not take me long to decide that there was only one project I should pursue. I was shocked by the great difference between media reporting and the reality on the ground. There was a story here to be told.

I ask you to suspend judgment of this book until the end. The desperate situation which is the individual reality of each Palestinian in the West Bank may be at odds with your current interpretation. However, this book is not intended to be a polemic. I have used skills developed while studying history and practising law, prior to becoming a photojournalist, to deliver what I believe is a fair interpretation of the current situation in the West Bank.

My primary resource for this book was the testimony of ordinary Palestinians whom I met whilst travelling around and I have included sections of my interviews with many of them in it. The interviewees include a dentist, lawyer and bank clerk, students, farmers and mothers. They are the substance of Palestinian society whose voice is rarely heard. Their aspirations are much the same as any other people around the world – to live in freedom and peace and to protect their families. They, however, face a desperate situation, not of their making. The stranglehold which Israel has over the West Bank is so tight and all encompassing that the issues raised in this book affect most Palestinian families. It is therefore inevitable that some interviews are relevant to several chapters. In most cases I have decided not to split them between such chapters, partly to emphasize this point.

I have decided to limit the scope of this book to the West Bank because it is here that any solution to the conflict will be found. Gaza is, of course, extremely important to the 1.5 million desperate Palestinians imprisoned within its walls but the West Bank makes up 94.2% of the Occupied Palestinian Territories, and if the Palestinians lose the battle here, their dreams of a state will be gone forever. In the last few years Israel has found it convenient to focus the world's attention on Gaza while quickly and efficiently manufacturing a new reality in the West Bank. This book seeks to redress the balance. Finally, I have also decided not to include interviews with Israeli settlers in this book. The approximate 450,000 Israeli settlers in East Jerusalem and the West Bank have been imported contrary to international law and as such they have no legal standing. To give them a voice would inevitably imply that their opinions and circumstances should carry equal weight.

Palestine and the media

One of my primary motivations for undertaking this project was to address the void between mainstream media coverage of the conflict and reality on the ground. For a number of reasons, elaborated on below, the media in the UK and more so in the US serves its public poorly in this area.

Some might point to Jewish ownership interests and managerial representation influencing the editorial line. This certainly occurs. The Jewish contribution to the arts, business and society in general in the West has been considerable but this success has resulted in their disproportionate representation at the higher levels of society. Western Jews often hold an overly romanticized view of Israel as a pioneer state, under constant threat, where intrepid Jews have made the desert bloom. Given Israel's constant reinforcement of this image and its promotion of Israel as a refuge from a future Holocaust, and the Jewish community's close cultural ties, it is not surprising that many Western Jews feel a need to defend Israel. Many others are as oblivious to the real facts as the next man or woman and in the absence of a powerful counterbalance take such statements as fact.

There are, however, much more obvious reasons why reporting tends to be skewed in Israel's favour. Firstly, over the years the Israeli government has developed a formidable PR machine. After any incident it is able to offer spokesmen and women to present the Israeli position. As it initiates most military contacts, it can also plan in advance. The Palestinians do not have this level of organization and cannot react as quickly. Additionally, Israel's unique position as a state of immigrants means that it is able to recruit Jewish spokespeople originating from the relevant news organizations' target audiences. The average British viewer will subconsciously feel more of an affinity with a white Israeli with a British accent than with a Palestinian Arab.

The media in general is also, like politicians and most other people in public life, extremely reluctant to criticize Israel. There are a large number of very well organized Jewish pressure groups which react to any publicity that could be seen as critical of Israel or of benefit to the Palestinians. The weight of complaints and the potentially adverse publicity that they can generate has created an atmosphere of political correctness. Legitimate criticism of Israel is soon portrayed as anti-Israeli bias, which can then be linked to anti-semitism. Few organizations, governments and public figures are prepared to stand up and tell the truth when the subject is peripheral to their audience's main interests and the backlash could be severe. Even an organization with as high journalistic standards as the BBC largely restricts itself to reporting the positions of both sides. It refrains from making any editorial assessment of the validity of such positions or highlighting injustices, something which it feels free to do with less politically sensitive areas like Zimbabwe.

Studies have shown a shift in terminology during the course of the occupation. The media has increasingly moved away from using the term "occupied" in favour of words like "disputed", suggesting that Israel has some legal claim on West Bank land. Occupied East Jerusalem is represented simply as part of Jerusalem, giving the viewer the impression that it is part of Israel. Whilst in most cases this can be put down to uninformed or lazy journalism, it seriously impacts on the audience's ability to comprehend an already confusing picture.

This confusion stems in part from the insidious nature of the conflict. The nature of modern media demands news events that can be portrayed well visually, and which can be understood quickly and easily. In the context of Palestine, this results in coverage of violence and its aftermath, demonstrations and funerals, and, occasionally, the Wall. Gaza has remained the dominant news item from the Occupied Territories since Israel's evacuation of settlements there in 2005. In fact, as this book will show, this suits Israel as it takes the world's eye off Israel's policies of annexation, imprisonment and ethnic cleansing in the West Bank. The reality is that the effects of many of Israel's policies in the West Bank are seen at an individual level – a family loses its land or decides it is time to emigrate, a business closes or a young man is put in prison. None of these events are in themselves newsworthy but together when repeated in large numbers they have a very real effect. Analysis of such effect is, however, impossible in a two-minute news item and therefore coverage does not reach the general public and is limited to the area of special interest news, where the target audience is those who often already have some level of consciousness of the situation.

Finally, I think too much trust is often given to journalistic reports. In the world of modern media, when deadlines are tight and budgets are strained, media organizations are in a weaker position to verify the accuracy of the reports they run. Some organizations retain very high standards whereas others take less care. As a small example, I spent

Busy commuter road in East Jerusalem. The tri-lingual sign belies the fact that the road is off-limits to the 90% of West Bank Palestinians who do not have Jerusalem residency status.

Christmas Eve 2006 in Bethlehem and was interested to see a piece on its desperate situation on a major American news network that evening. It stated that only one solitary tourist visited the Nativity Church grotto that day. This was news to me as I had to scrum down with a coach load of Filipinos to get in. I spoke to my hotel proprietor who was also featured and he said the TV crew had actually visited the previous week. The story was in essence true – I met more journalists than tourists there – but the TV crew had manipulated the facts to add drama to its story.

Anti-semitism and the Holocaust

Anti-semitism is a hatred of Jews as a race which in modern times has most horrifically found its expression in Europe, not the Middle East. There is, of course, a great deal of hostility towards Jews in the Arab world but this was triggered and fomented by the mass immigration of Jews into Palestine, the creation of Israel and Israel's subsequent treatment of the Palestinians. Islam in fact has a far better record of tolerating other religions than Christianity. For centuries prior to 1900, Muslim and Christian Arabs, and Jews, lived side by side under the rule of the Ottoman Empire, often worshipping together at the same shrines. Unfortunately, the emigration to Israel of whole populations of Jews from Arab states in which they had lived for centuries helped to polarize Arabs and Jews. The exploitation of the Palestinian issue by leaders of Muslim states (most recently President Ahmadinejad of Iran) for their own ends has further widened this divide and encouraged a hatred of Jews amongst their people. In contrast however, Palestinians are among the most educated of Arab peoples, and most are careful to distinguish the actions of the Israeli government, the Israeli Defence Force (IDF) and settlers from ordinary Jewish Israelis. Any hatred they bear is born out of the regime which oppresses them.

One risks the accusation of pedantry if one points out that Arabs are semitic too. However, this is important, even though the term is linguistic and not racial in origin. Israel is pursuing a policy of separation and differentiation from the Palestinians on the basis that Jews and Arabs cannot live together. However, prior to the first *intifada*, a widescale and largely non-violent uprising against Israeli occupation between 1987 and 1991, huge numbers of Palestinians in the West Bank were employed in Israel. The infrastructure of Israel, including many settlements, was built with Palestinian labour. The relationship was the colonial model of master and servant but the peoples coexisted. Hebrew is very similar to Arabic and so many Palestinians are bilingual. Indeed, a Palestinian recently went so far as to say to me: "Arabs and Jews, we are the same."

The Palestinians' desire for a state stems not from a deep sense of nationalism but a desire to control their own destiny. Arabs in general do not have a strong allegiance to their states. In part this is because the boundaries of these states were arbitrarily drawn by the British and French governments and because their inhabitants have been denied democratic government. However, it is also because, for most Arabs, their God and their family are their primary sources of obligation. Of course, many Palestinian refugees would prefer it if Israel did not exist, as they could then return to the land on which they or their fathers were born. However, it does exist and most Palestinians accept its permanence. What they truly desire is to be treated fairly – for Jews and Arabs to be allowed the same access to land, to water, to life.

In contrast, Zionism, the philosophy behind the creation of a Jewish state in Palestine, was, and Israel remains, heavily influenced by the philosophy of nationalism and racial purity prevalent in central and eastern Europe in the early twentieth century and which ultimately found horrific expression in Nazi Germany. Anti-semitism was seen by some in the Zionist movement as a natural consequence of the mixing of races. The obvious solution was to create a national entity exclusively for Jews. It also offered an opportunity to maintain Jewish culture which was under threat from increasing secularization of Jews in western society. While the doctrine of racial purity was defeated in Europe intellectually and physically by the Allies in World War II (although it reappeared in the Balkans late in the century), it is perpetuated in Israel, "the Jewish state". Palestinians with Israeli citizenship remain second-class citizens within Israel, tolerated in the absence of any other solution.

The Zionist mission to colonize Palestine was well under way before World War II, the first meeting of the World Zionist Organization taking place in 1897. However, following the creation of Israel the Holocaust became Zionism's justification and a bulwark against criticism of its actions. The Holocaust has been described by some commentators as the state religion because of its all pervading effect on Israeli society. It is not uncommon, however, for Palestinians to deny the Holocaust took place or at least question the numbers killed. This reflects badly upon them. It should be remembered though that it was Europeans and not Arabs who committed the atrocities and many Palestinians feel that they are paying the price for Europe's crime. The history of the Holocaust is embedded in Western society and reinforced by education, media and Hollywood. It is not therefore surprising that people living on a different continent without such influences, many of whom have access only to state-controlled media, should have a much lower level of consciousness. Also, it is perhaps understandable that there is a degree of suspicion and disbelief given Israel's lack of concern in violating the very laws established to try to prevent atrocities of the type committed against the Jews by the Nazis. To Palestinians it seems manifestly unjust that their oppressor should be granted such a trump card, enabling it to influence western governments and silence criticism of its actions against them. As one Palestinian said to me, "You can't expect someone who has had the shit kicked out of him to have sympathy for his attacker."

Young Palestinian boy learning to walk, with the Dome of the Rock and Al-Aqsa mosque in the background, East Jerusalem.

The 7th-century Al-Aqsa mosque is the third most holy mosque in the world. The first two are in Mecca, Saudi Arabia, making Jerusalem the second most important city for Muslims. The Dome and Al-Aqsa mosque are built on the Haram al-Sharif, known to Jews as Temple Mount because it is believed to be the site of the temple of Solomon, King of Israel and son of David. The Second (and last) Temple was destroyed by the Romans in 70 AD.

What Did We Do To Deserve This?

Introduction

Israel occupied the West Bank, including East Jerusalem, and the Gaza Strip (as well as the Syrian Golan Heights and part of the Sinai peninsula) during the Six Day War between 5th and 10th June 1967. This event is known by Palestinians as the *naksa*. Forty years on, with the exception of the Sinai lands which were returned to Egypt under the 1978 Camp David Accords, Israel retains control of these territories. The occupation of the West Bank and Gaza (the "Occupied Territories") was recognized as illegal by the United Nations in Security Council Resolution 242 in November 1967 and, over the years, the international community, led by the US, has sought to reach a settlement between Israel and the Palestinians. However, the latest "peace process" has long since stalled and a Palestinian state now looks further away than ever. Western politicians still stick to the mantra of a two-state solution incorporating a viable Palestinian state, but have events on the ground overtaken diplomacy? Has Israel won the war and ended any possibility of Palestinian nationhood?

Palestine is a geographical area incorporating Israel, the West Bank and Gaza, bounded by the River Jordan to the east, the Mediterranean Sea to the west, Sinai to the south and, less distinctly, Syria and Lebanon to the north. I use the word "Palestine" in this book when referring to the area which comprises Israel and the West Bank, which should not be confused with the areas of the West Bank for which the Palestinian Authority currently has responsibility. The name Palestine was first applied to the general area by the Romans but more specifically to the territory described above by the Arab rulers in the seventh century. It was recognized as a distinct political unit by the League of Nations in 1923 following Great Britain's appointment as mandatory power (the governing authority). In 1947 the United Nations voted to divide Palestine into Jewish and Arab states, with Jerusalem to be placed under international stewardship. On the cessation of the British mandate in May 1948, the Jewish leader, David Ben Gurion, declared independence and Israel was born. During the fighting which followed, known as the 1948 War, Israel annexed territory allocated to the Arab state and West Jerusalem, increasing its share of Palestine from 56% to 78%. The remaining 22%, the West Bank and Gaza Strip, fell under the control of Jordan and Egypt respectively, depriving the Palestinians of an independent state. However, despite this division and the forced flight of hundreds of thousands of Palestinians in 1948 from their lands, and Israel's separation of the two peoples by its system of walls and other barriers, Palestine remains economically and geographically a distinct unit. Over a million Palestinians remain within Israeli borders and hold Israeli citizenship while Israel's policies in the West Bank since occupation have served to integrate much of its land (but not its 2.5 million people) within the state of Israel. In Palestinian hearts, Palestine is indivisible. Similarly, most Jewish Israelis consider the West Bank to be an integral part of the state of Israel.

Much has been made of Israel's 2005 "withdrawal" from the Gaza Strip. This has been a masterpiece of public relations work by the Israeli government, which has made full use of the media to publicize its "concessions". Reality is somewhat different. Gaza is a barren place with little water and a population of 1.4 million Palestinians, 75% of whom are refugees. It makes up only 5.8% of the total land mass of the Occupied Territories, the remainder being the West Bank. It was a headache for the Israeli government. The number of soldiers getting killed in attacks by Palestinians in defending only 8,000 settlers presented a political problem. By withdrawing behind the walls it has erected around Gaza it can claim it is no longer in occupation while still controlling Gaza's borders and attacking targets in Gaza from within its own borders and from the air. Meanwhile, Israel has increased the pace of settlement building in the West Bank and has taken the opportunity to complete the Wall while western politicians' and the media's attention has been distracted. Between January and September 2005, around 11,000 new settlers arrived in the West Bank and in July 2005 alone, Israel seized more land in the West Bank than it surrendered in Gaza. Indeed, Ariel Sharon justified the withdrawal to his people on the basis that the world would permit Israel to retain its settlements in the West Bank if it removed those in Gaza.

Although the West Bank remains the real battlefield in the Palestinian struggle for a state, this is only in a figurative sense. The relationship between Israel and the Palestinians is often described as a "conflict", a term I too use from time to time for want of a more accurate one. However, this is misleading as it implies two distinct entities with the means to sustain armed action. The correct legal relationship is one of occupation. In practice, it has been colonial while increasingly it is becoming one of apartheid. In physical terms, Israel is holding down an unwilling population that, by various methods, violent and non-violent, and with massively inferior resources, has resisted such subjugation from within the *de facto* borders of Israel.

The most recent national manifestation of Palestinian resistance, the second *intifada,* is now over. West Bank Palestinians are tired and the vast majority just wish to be left alone to live their lives in peace. The armed struggle has ended, or is at least in abeyance, awaiting a new generation of resistance. The grip that Israel has over the West Bank is total and unrelenting. The Wall, which has greedily devoured Palestinian land and isolated Palestinian communities, is the most obvious manifestation of this power but Israel's hold extends to every aspect of life – movement, religious worship, land use, business, the environment, health, education and marriage. The daily humiliations and degrading treatment seem calculated to drive Palestinians out of the West Bank, deprive them of their identity and remove any possibility of a Palestinian state. The tragedy is that this policy is succeeding.

With the tacit approval of the US government, illegal settlement building, accelerated greatly since the mid 1990s, has populated the West Bank with approximately 450,000 Israelis, 180,000 of these in East Jerusalem. Through settlements, road networks and other confiscated and closed areas, Israel controls large areas of the West Bank and many Israeli politicians strive for much more. The enormous settlements of Ariel and Ma'ale Adumim stretch into the West Bank like great fingers dividing it into three. The Israeli road network which links settlements with each other and Israel splinters the land that remains, imprisoning the Palestinians within ever-shrinking enclaves. The word "prison" is used regularly in this book to describe the areas within which West Bank Palestinians are being confined. This is partly because it is accurate but also because it is the word Palestinians on the ground themselves use most frequently to describe their situation.

Israel has successfully manoeuvred the media into accepting that the Wall – which in places cuts 24 miles across the Green Line (the 1948 armistice line and Israel's internationally accepted eastern border) into the West Bank – will constitute the new border between Israel and a Palestinian state. It is widely assumed that the great powers are simply waiting for Israel to complete the Wall before giving their blessing to a two-state solution dictated by its path, thereby permitting Israel to annex 10% of the West Bank including East Jerusalem. This is complacency in the extreme. Since 1967 Israeli governments have held a consistent policy towards the West Bank based on the Allon Plan of that year. The policy dictates that Israel must secure and maintain under its control large swathes of West Bank land. The reality is that the Israeli military and settler presence in the West Bank is deeply embedded. A new, invisible wall is rising in the Jordan Valley. It is clear that Israel intends to annex at an absolute minimum the 40% of the West Bank which it already directly controls while maintaining indirect control of the remainder.

The Israeli government believes that the US's involvement in Iraq and its favourable administration have given it a window of opportunity in which it can ensure its annexation of these areas, and possibly enforce a "settlement" which the international community will endorse, and which will remove the Palestinian cause from the world agenda for the foreseeable future. The speed with which Israel is implementing its unilateral settlement is frightening. The Wall is all but complete. Palestinian land is being devoured and its population being cleansed as I write. International law is flouted at every turn. War crimes abound. Meanwhile, the world turns its back.

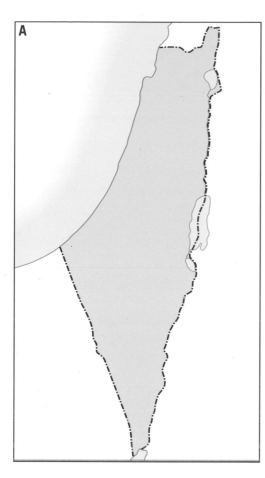

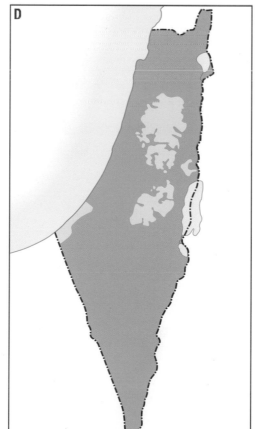

Destroying the Two-State Solution

A Pre-1948
100% of Historic Palestine

B 1947 UN Partion Plan
48% of Historic Palestine

C 1967 Pre-Occupation Border
22% of Historic Palestine

D The Wall (2004)
12% of Historic Palestine

Jewish Control/Israel

Historic Palestine/Arab Control

Proposed international zone
incorporating Jerusalem and
Bethlehem

A problem of our making

Britain and the US are largely responsible for the situation which the Palestinians find themselves in. One cannot blame individual citizens of these countries for the mistakes and broken promises of their predecessors or perhaps even for the foreign policy decisions of the governments which they themselves elect. I believe they do, however, have a collective, moral responsibility to attempt to address the consequences of these actions and omissions where they are still being felt today. Although the two powers' history in the Middle East is widely understood and resented in the Arab world, it is less well known in the West. I will therefore briefly set it out.

Prior to World War I, Arabia (including Palestine) was part of the ailing Ottoman Empire. The Ottoman government allied with Germany during the war, thus presenting a threat to Great Britain's strategic interests in Suez and the Gulf. The British therefore approached Sharif Hussein, an Arab leader, to determine which side the Ottoman Empire's Arab subjects would support. Several promises of support for the Arabs were made, culminating in a letter from the British High Commissioner in Egypt in October 1915 pledging British support for Arab independence. Several areas were excluded from this commitment but not Palestine. Consequently, the Arabs allied with the British and instigated the Arab Revolt against the Ottomans (1916–18). Britain, however, was also negotiating with France, resulting in the Sykes-Picot agreement of 1916 whereby the two countries secretly agreed to partition the Middle East between them, leaving only the area comprising present-day Saudi Arabia and North Yemen independent.

Compounding this betrayal, in 1917 the British foreign secretary issued a letter, the Balfour Declaration, to a leading British Zionist Jew stating that his government viewed "with favour the establishment in Palestine of a National Home for the Jewish people, and [would] use their best endeavours to facilitate the achievement of this object". This was despite the presence of a massive Arab majority in Palestine. In 1922 the British census revealed there were only 84,000 Jews in Palestine compared with 670,000 Palestinians. However, the members of the British government saw a strategic interest in a Jewish Palestine annexed to the British Empire and were also sympathetic to the Zionist cause. Herbert Samuel, a Jew, first proposed it but many of the non-Jews in the government saw the return of the Jews to Zion as a romantic fulfilment of Old Testament prophecy. They also wanted the support of world Jewry and believed that the Zionist project would help to maintain US interest in World War I. Jews were also viewed as part of western civilization whereas the Arabs were seen as a subject race. While the Balfour Declaration is a footnote in British history, it set in motion a chain of events resulting in the creation of Israel, Palestinian dispossession, exile and subjugation, and the Israeli-Palestinian troubles.

A further declaration in November 1918 stated that the British and French governments were committed to establishing essentially democratic, self-governing nations in the Middle East even though they had no intention of honouring this. In March 1920 the General Syrian Congress, an elected body, proclaimed the independence of Syria and Palestine. Britain and France then rushed to convene the League of Nations, which rejected the declaration and divided the area into mandates including a British-controlled Palestinian mandate which carried with it an obligation to enforce the Balfour Declaration. Britain had not only broken its repeated promises of independence to the Arabs but committed to the Palestinians' ultimate subjugation to Jewish rule.

While running the mandate, British policy towards Jewish immigration varied from time to time. However, by its cessation in 1948 Britain had allowed the Jewish population in Palestine to increase to roughly 600,000. Britain permitted the Jews to build the mechanisms of a state within the mandate including an elected body raising taxes, and an underground army. They also engaged Jewish forces in putting down the Arab Revolt of 1936 to 1938. In a white paper in 1938, to pacify the Palestinians during World War II, the British government promised to limit Jewish immigration and move towards the establishment of a Palestinian state within ten years. However, by the end of the war Britain had lost control of events and the creation of Israel had become inevitable.

This did not, however, absolve them from all responsibility for the mandate. Britain had announced, in September 1947, its intention to give up the mandate on 15 May 1948. In the month and a half before withdrawal, Britain took no responsibility for enforcement of law and order. While perhaps reasonable in the context of a withdrawal, the fact that British forces failed to intervene to stop Jewish forces committing acts of ethnic cleansing is shameful. Infamously, the British commander in Haifa withdrew his forces from a buffer zone between the two communities and allowed the Jewish Carmeli Brigade to put to flight most of its 55,000 remaining Palestinian inhabitants. In some instances they provided positive assistance to Jewish forces, giving them valuable documents, and in one case even disarmed Palestinians, promising to protect them, and then failed to do so.

As a fledgling state, surrounded by hostile Arab countries and engaged in frequent wars against them, Israel's survival was perhaps not always certain. However, with support from the US, it has now developed its military capabilities to the point where it is the fifth mightiest military power in the world. Aided by the US, Britain and France it has developed nuclear weapons and is today the fourth largest nuclear power. It also benefits from secure peace treaties with two of its former enemies, Egypt and Jordan. The fact is that Israel is now secure and has been since the 1970s.

Israel still, however, plays the vulnerability card. It encourages the view that Arabs wish to see it driven into the sea to help it garner support in the West and justify its actions against Palestinians. Since the 1970s the US has responded wholeheartedly and supported Israel unwaveringly. Since 1982, it has vetoed 32 UN Security Council Resolutions critical of Israel, more than the total number of vetoes cast by all the other Security Council members put together. Meanwhile the US gives between US$3 and US$5 billion in "aid" to Israel every year, more than it gives to all of sub-Saharan Africa. Much of it is in the form of state-of-the-art weapons, for example, Apache helicopters, which are used against the Palestinians. The US has also failed to operate as an honest broker in negotiations with the Palestinians, consistently aligning itself with Israel.

The Jewish lobby in the US is so sophisticated that it has succeeded in emasculating Congress with respect to Israeli-related issues. The American-Israeli Public Affairs Committee (AIPAC) is acknowledged as one of the most effective lobbies in Washington, keeping records of all statements on the Middle East made by Congress members and prospective candidates. It counters fiercely any comments which could be seen as pro-Palestinian or anti-Israeli through its media contacts. There are hundreds of smaller pro-Israeli groups which mount letter-writing campaigns in response to such comments and contribute funds to candidates seeking election to seats held by Congress members who dare make such comments. The majority therefore keep quiet even though there is increasing understanding of the validity of the Palestinian cause. AIPAC's influence extends into other areas of American life, particularly universities. It has worked to establish pro-Israeli groups which protest against tutors and speakers who it perceives as expressing pro-Palestinian views. Even American Jews are targeted. Zionism has become an article of faith and it is considered heresy to dissent. In essence, the lobby's purpose is to make the expression of pro-Palestinian views in American society unacceptable and ease Israel's interests by, for example, encouraging US aid.

This influence extended to the Oval Office even before Israel was created. President Truman was advised by his military and diplomatic aides to delay recognition of Israel in 1948 until the Arab states could be consulted but he rejected their advice, instead acting on the recommendation of a close pro-Zionist, Jewish friend, fearing a backlash from Jewish Americans. Jews and evangelical Christians (who support Zionism because they see the return of Jews to Israel biblically as a precursor of the Day of Judgement) make up only 20% of voters but they have a disproportionate effect in elections because of their high contribution and turnout levels. The Washington Post once estimated that democratic presidential candidates depend on Jewish supporters to supply as much as 60% of their campaign money. This influence was felt again in 1967 when President Johnson accepted Israel's argument that it should be allowed to keep the West Bank as a bargaining chip. The extent of Israeli influence is shown by the lengths to which that administration went to in order to cover up Israel's attack on the USS *Liberty* during the Six Day War.

In Britain, with restrictions on large donations and prohibition of foreign funding, the relatively wealthy Jewish community is a valuable source of funding for political parties. The minister for the Middle East, Kim Howells, used to be the Chairman of Labour Friends of Israel. Lord Levy, formerly the Labour Party's chief fundraiser and Middle East envoy, happens to be Jewish. At the 2006 Conservative Friends of Israel (CFI) fringe meeting at the Conservative Party Conference, both the leader, David Cameron, and the shadow defence secretary gave speeches thanking the group for its support. A director of CFI recently claimed that over 80% of the Conservative parliamentary party were members. Unfortunately short-term political expediency is always likely to win out over worthy long-term initiatives.

Up until the current suspension of aid, European governments have continually assuaged their guilt by pumping aid money into the West Bank to support Palestinians, but by doing so they have relieved Israel of its obligations to provide support to Palestinians under the Geneva Convention. At the same time they license the sale of arms to Israel which are used against Palestinians, and buy Israeli weapons. When Israel destroys the buildings they fund, no action is taken. The EU continues to allow the import of Israeli goods under a treaty which permits the imposition of sanctions against Israel in the event of human rights breaches. War crimes legislation positively obliges countries to seek out and prosecute perpetrators but these obligations are ignored.

Despite George W. Bush's commitment to a Palestinian state made in June 2002, under his administration US foreign policy in the Middle East has more heavily than ever been influenced by Israel. Israel has implicitly been given the green light to implement its unilateral solution in the West Bank. Impossible preconditions to talks and aid are required of the Hamas government whereas Israel's actions and omissions go unquestioned. By supplying weapons to Fatah groups and planning a package of support to that party worth US$86 million, the US government has been working to overthrow Hamas, subverting the democratic process and risking the outbreak of a Palestinian civil war. The International Court of Justice's ruling against Israel's routing of the Wall and continuing occupation, issued in July 2004, has been ignored. Meanwhile, George Bush has undermined international law and forty years of UN resolutions, negotiated agreements and international pressure concerning Israeli settlement of the West Bank by recognizing "new realities on the ground, including already existing major Israeli population centers". The European Union, Russia and even the UN have continued to acquiesce to the US approach.

It is not surprising that Palestinians feel they have been consistently betrayed by the West.

Israeli checkpoint at
Al-Khadr between East
Jerusalem and Hebron

PART 1:
CALIBRATING TO REALITY

1 The myth of a state

The Palestinians have a president. They also have a pluralistic, parliamentary democracy. They do not, however, have a country to govern. Ironically it was the mechanism that established this political system, the Oslo Accords (explained below), which could well have destroyed any opportunity of an independent state for the Palestinians.

Governments around the world entertain Palestinian president Mahmoud Abbas. The four sponsors of the Roadmap – the US, the European Union, Russia and the UN (known as the Quartet) – occasionally suggest that there is still mileage in this latest peace process. Meanwhile, Israel continues full steam ahead with its unilateral settlement. The impression given is that although times are difficult, all parties are committed to a two-state solution. On the ground, however, there is no evidence that Israel shares this view.

The Zionists who were the founding fathers of Israel always viewed the West Bank (known to Israelis by the biblical names of Judea and Samaria) as part of Israel. Israel's first Prime Minister, David Ben Gurion, made it clear when accepting the principle of partition in 1947 that it would only be a staging post on the road to an Israeli state covering all of Palestine. Prior to the 1948 War, Ben Gurion secretly agreed with King Abdullah of Jordan, who possessed the only well-trained army in the Arab world, that Jordan would refrain from fighting the Israeli army in exchange for Israel's acquiescence to Jordan's annexation of the West Bank. However, he reneged on this deal once Israel's superiority became apparent and the Jordanian army had to fight to retain its control of this area in the war. Israel's invasion of the West Bank in 1967 was largely a defensive measure in time of war, albeit a war which it was fully prepared for and in which it struck the first blows. However, once occupied, initial indecision over the fate of the West Bank soon gave way to a decision to retain it as a buffer pending the negotiation of peace treaties with its Arab neighbours and then to a policy of colonization.

The Israeli government's conversion to a "two-state solution" was dictated by demographics. The number of Palestinians in Palestine is approaching the total number of Jews and with the higher Palestinian birth rate it may not be long before Palestinians outnumber Jews. Israel is in a bind. Israel describes itself as "Jewish and democratic". It wants to keep the West Bank land but does not want to incorporate its Palestinian population. Accepting them would make Israel unsustainable as a "Jewish" state unless Palestinians were given lesser voting rights, compromising Israel's democratic status. A mechanism had to be established whereby the Palestinians could be portrayed as governing themselves, thereby releasing Israel from responsibility for them and appeasing the international community, but which in reality allowed Israel to maintain control.

Palestinians queuing to cross the Wall into East Jerusalem from Qalandia. Under international law East Jerusalem and Qalandia (together with the rest of the West Bank) form one integral territory.

Israel has therefore rapidly built a barrier – one which would not have looked out of place on a cold war, international border – around the entire West Bank (excluding the River Jordan and Dead Sea to which Palestinians are already denied access). In this book I refer to it by its most commonly used name, the "Wall", although in some places it takes the form of a high security fence. To the West this is portrayed as a natural precursor to a two state solution. The Wall is built entirely on the Palestinian side of the Green Line and snakes around to separate Palestinians from their land. In places it cuts deep into the West Bank to include Israeli settlements. Its manufactured route is demonstrated by its length – 662 kiilometres – over twice that of the Green Line. In all, 10% of West Bank land including East Jerusalem has effectively been annexed behind the Wall. Its purpose is to restrict the movement of, and essentially imprison, West Bank Palestinians. Palestinians must cross on foot through high-security checkpoints if they wish to travel between Jerusalem and the West Bank and may only do so if they have a permit. In contrast, Israelis have their own crossing points which resemble motorway toll stations rather than border crossings, through which they can pass freely by car to the West Bank settlements.

Israel is also in the process of annexing the Jordan valley, west of the river which it sees as its eastern border. It has used the security and administrative powers given to it under the Oslo Accords to divide Palestinian areas into what are essentially Bantustans (unconnected enclaves with limited self-governance created by the South African government in the apartheid era). Palestinians are restricted from using major roads which, together with new settler roads, have become tools of separation. This lack of continuity of land makes the Palestinian Authority's role very difficult. It has to manage operations in unconnected areas between which its employees have no guarantee of transit. Management and construction of basic infrastructure is subject to Israeli permissions when it extends beyond town boundaries. Electricity and water are supplied by Israeli companies. Palestinians are prevented from building in areas administered by Israel, bottling them up in existing urban areas. All in all, the lands administered by the Palestinian Authority are a very long way from constituting a "viable" Palestinian state.

The Oslo Accords

The 1993 and 1995 Oslo Accords provided for the withdrawal of Israeli forces from parts of the West Bank and affirmed the right of Palestinians to self government in major centres of Palestinian population through the creation of the Palestinian Authority (the "PA"). As a temporary measure, the Accords divided the West Bank into three jurisdictional areas: Area A where the PA had administrative and security control; Area B where the PA had administrative control and Israel had security control; and Area C where Israel had administrative and security control. The Palestinian Authority's jurisdiction was, however,

restricted to internal administrative issues – Jerusalem, settlements, refugees, borders, Israeli citizens, military areas and foreign affairs were all off-limits.

On the face of it, the Palestinians had negotiated a stepping stone towards the end of the occupation and the creation of a Palestinian state. In fact the Accords proved to be a triumph for Israel. Prior to the Accords, Israel was universally recognized as an occupying power. It was obliged to withdraw from the West Bank under Resolution 242 and had agreed to enter negotiations based on the principles of that resolution under the Camp David Accords of 1978. It had also failed to give the Palestinians humanitarian support required under the 4th Geneva Convention.

The creation of the PA, however, allowed Israel to hand over to it responsibility for the vast majority of West Bank Palestinians. The Accords imposed on the PA "all liabilities and obligations arising with regard to acts or omissions" which occurred under Israeli occupation. Israel was given authority to maintain troops in areas subject to Israeli security control, thereby legitimizing its military and civilian presence, while retaining responsibility for the overall security of Israelis, setting in place the mechanisms of apartheid. Successive Israeli and US governments have applied pressure on the PA to crack down on Palestinian militants which essentially turned the Palestinian security forces into a division of the Israeli forces, protecting their own occupiers. Meanwhile any militant attack that evaded the Palestinian security forces' net was used by Israel as an excuse for refusing to negotiate a final settlement.

Yitzhak Rabin, the Israeli Prime Minister, may have genuinely intended to make peace but he was assassinated by a settler soon after the Accords were signed and was succeeded by leaders determined to destroy the Oslo process. The Accord's five-year interim period came and went without a final agreement and ultimately most Palestinian gains were clawed back during Israel's reoccupation of Palestinian areas under Operation Defensive Shield in 2002 which destroyed much of the infrastructure of the PA, and the Palestinian economy. The Palestinian political structure of President and legislative council remains but it may do the Palestinians more harm than good. These institutions give the impression of a state and disguise the continuing fact of occupation. Under the control of Fatah, historically the leading Palestinian party, the PA appeared increasingly subject to Israeli and US influence. As a peace process, the Oslo Accords are consigned to history. Its legacy remains on the ground, however, imprisoning Palestinians. As American academic, Norman Finkelstein, states:

"The US and Israel seized on this opportune moment to recruit the already venal and now desperate Palestinian leadership … as surrogates of Israeli power. This was the real meaning of the Oslo Accord … to create a Palestinian Bantustan by dangling before Arafat and the PLO the perquisites of power and privilege."

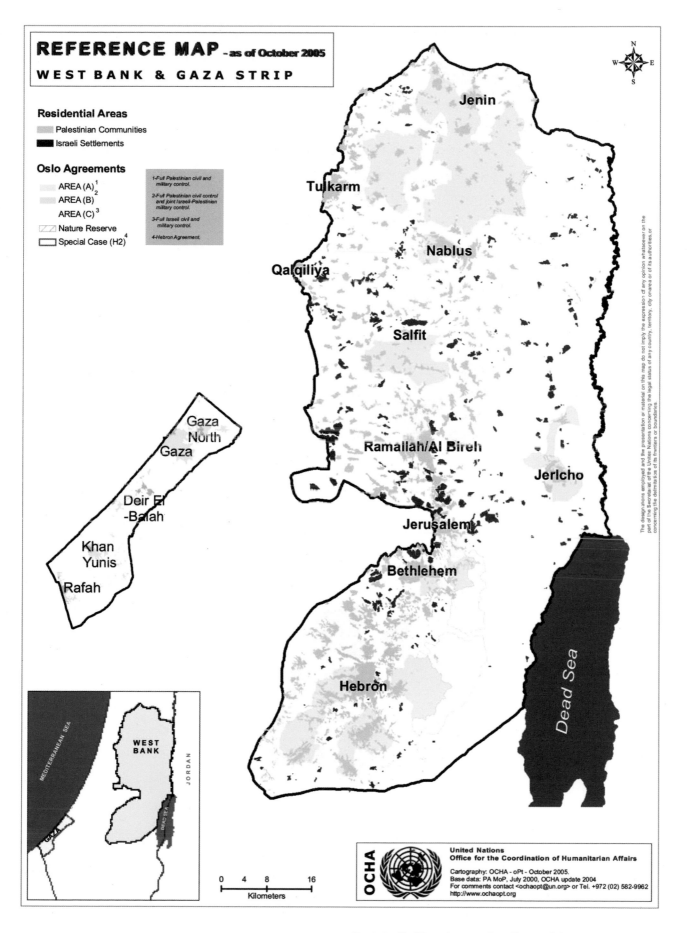

REFERENCE MAP – as of October 2005
WEST BANK & GAZA STRIP

Residential Areas
- Palestinian Communities
- Israeli Settlements

Oslo Agreements
- AREA (A)[1]
- AREA (B)[2]
- AREA (C)[3]
- Nature Reserve
- Special Case (H2)[4]

1-Full Palestinian civil and military control.

2-Full Palestinian civil control and joint Israeli-Palestinian military control.

3-Full Israeli civil and military control.

4-Hebron Agreement.

Jenin

Tulkarm

Nablus

Qalqiliya

Salfit

Ramallah/Al Bireh

Jericho

Jerusalem

Bethlehem

Hebron

Dead Sea

Gaza North
Gaza
Deir El -Balah
Khan Yunis
Rafah

MEDITERRANEAN SEA
WEST BANK
JORDAN
GAZA
DEAD SEA

The design shown employed and the presentation or material on this map do not imply the expression of any opinion whatsoever on the part of the Secretariat of the United Nations concerning the legal status of any country, territory, city or area or of its authorities, or concerning the delimitation of its frontiers or boundaries.

0 4 8 16
Kilometers

United Nations
Office for the Coordination of Humanitarian Affairs

Cartography: OCHA - oPt - October 2005.
Base data: PA MoP, July 2000, OCHA update 2004
For comments contact <ochaopt@un.org> or Tel. +972 (02) 582-9962
http://www.ochaopt.org

On 4th January 2007, I was sitting in a hotel in Ramallah when I heard helicopters and shooting outside. Flicking through the TV channels, I hit an Arabic-language channel which was showing live coverage of an Israeli raid only 500 metres from my hotel. The IDF press briefing that followed stated that this was a "routine" action to arrest militants. The Israeli Prime Minister, Ehud Olmert, said that it was "unfortunate" that four Palestinian civilians (including one child) had been killed. The military briefing made its way onto CNN and BBC World without a Palestinian response.

In some ways it was normal. The Israeli Defence Force mounts actions of this sort daily across the West Bank. However, Israel generally treats Ramallah with a lighter touch than other West Bank cities. It is close to Jerusalem and Israeli influence and Israel has encouraged its development as the centre of the Palestinian Authority. Many NGOs (non-governmental organizations) are based there and it feels less impoverished than other towns.

The raid took place just before the Israeli Prime Minister, Ehud Olmert, sat down with the Egyptian President to discuss the "peace process". Was this just a coincidence? Perhaps. However, for two hours Israeli armoured vehicles and bulldozers were pictured live on Arab satellite TV controlling Ramallah's main square, Al Minara, and destroying the town's vegetable market and nearby vehicles. An Israeli helicopter fired on and killed the owner of a coffee stall in the square known by local Palestinians as the Father of Happiness for his good nature. The implication seemed clear. The Palestinians should not get their hopes up. Israel would remain in control.

The author

Israeli armoured vehicles and
bulldozers in Ramallah's main
square, live on Arabic TV.

"The Palestinian Authority lacks money. There are only two people in the council and both are unpaid. Our building was paid for by a UN/EU development programme but we can't afford to employ enough staff.

The Israelis don't consult with us. They are just interested in making it harder for us to live. We have only 70 rubbish containers for 2,000 people. The Israelis don't allow the PA to build recycling factories or create landfill sites, so we have to burn our rubbish. The smoke blows over Ramallah but we can't move the burning site. We have no sewerage system. We dig big holes near our houses instead. A US$1 million sewerage project funded by foreign donors was stopped by the Israelis because it needed to join with pipes from the jail and the settlement.

Rafat used to have 6,000 dunums [1,482 acres] of farmland. Now there are only 2,500 [617 acres] because of the settlement, military base, jail, road and wall. And most of that is in Area C so we can't use it for anything except farming. The Israelis built on the best place for farming in all of Palestine.

The settlement was built 25 years ago. Then there were two or three buildings. Now there are 20,000. Many houses are empty – Israelis build houses with long-term mortgages and buy several houses in different settlements as investments.

We are being strangled. There is no work. I have four sons with no jobs."

Abdul Hafifh Hassan, Mayor of Rafat, a village near Ramallah

Abdul Hafifh Hassan,
Mayor of Rafat council

Single-room dwelling in Nahallin, built on Palestinian land under Israeli administrative control (Area C under the Oslo Accords) to test whether the Israeli authorities will destroy it.

Palestinian dwelling in Area C
(Palestinian land administered by
Israel under the Oslo Accords)
subject to Israeli demolition order,
Jifflick, Jordan Valley

Fortified road between Jerusalem and Israeli settlements built on Palestinian land but for Israeli-only use. The road cuts across the Palestinian enclave of Bir Nabala (marked with a "7" on the map on page 79), leaving this tunnel as the only access point to the Palestinian village of Qalandia.

2 | **Transfer**

1948

> "People are not born to struggle; they are born to live. If life is made difficult and people have an opportunity elsewhere many will leave, although some will stay and fight."
>
> **Ghassan, Birzeit**

There are now roughly 200,000 Palestinian refugees in camps across the West Bank housing those too poor or proud to leave. Today, the camps consist of poorly built, concrete buildings which rise ever upward as the population expands. In total there are currently over 700,000 refugees in the territory. The first generation of refugees fled from areas of Palestine allocated to the Jews by the UN and which constituted Israel's original territory, or land annexed by Israel in 1948. There are still a good number of them alive, but their advanced years means these events will soon be beyond living memory.

There had been clashes between Palestinians and Jews from early in the 20th century as the number of Jews settling in Palestine increased. The Palestinians fully appreciated that the Jews intended to take Palestine for themselves and, as more and more Jews arrived, unrest increased culminating in the Palestinian Revolt in 1936. The revolt was firmly put down by British forces and its leaders exiled, and thereafter Palestinian resistance remained largely local and unorganized. In contrast, militarily, the Jews had superior numbers, arms and organization. The Haganah, their underground army, is estimated to have had 65,000 troops in 1946, many with battle experience from World War II. Splinter groups from the Haganah had been committing widespread terrorist attacks on British and Palestinian targets throughout the war.

The clashes became much more violent and widespread after World War II as large numbers of Jews arrived from Europe and after the British announced their intention to surrender the mandate. On the day the mandate ceased, David Ben Gurion declared Israel's independence and in response the surrounding Arab countries sent in 20,000 troops to engage the Jewish forces. Although the 1948 War is often portrayed as a great triumph for Israel, Israel's victory was never in doubt because of its secret agreement with Jordan. The small number and lack of organization of forces from other Arab countries meant they posed no real threat. With their leadership structure destroyed, there was also no real organized Palestinian response. Indeed, Jewish forces were able to implement Plan Dalet, their systematic ethnic cleansing of Palestinians, unhindered during the War. In implementing the plan, Jewish forces committed at least 24 atrocities, the most infamous being at Deir Yassin where 250 Palestinian civilians were killed. As a consequence of these attacks and the spread of stories about them (aided by Jewish loudhailers), over 700,000 Palestinians fled their villages in terror, leaving their homes and possessions behind. Where elderly and infirm remained, they were forced on to buses at gunpoint. In all, some 420 Palestinian villages were cleansed.

Mural, Deheisheh Refugee Camp,
Bethlehem

The concept of "transfer", the forced migration of Palestinians from Palestine to neighbouring Arab lands, had been discussed widely in Zionist circles in the preceding half century. David Ben Gurion and the other Israeli leaders fully appreciated that, on declaration of independence, Jews would be a minority within the lands allocated to them by the United Nations. The UN partition plan anticipated the Jewish state to have 507,780 Arabs and 499,020 Jews and at that point Jews only owned 7% of the land. The viability of a Jewish state would be fatally compromised if the Palestinians remained.

Most refugees expected their exile to be short lived – a matter of weeks or at most months until things calmed down or the Arab armies came to retake their territory. However, those who remain alive are now entering their 60th year as refugees. Under UN resolution 194 of December 1948, all UN-registered refugees (and their descendants) have a right to return to Palestine and reclaim their property or be compensated for their loss, at their choice. However, Israel stopped those who tried to return to their homes, killing between 2,700 and 5,000 Arab infiltrators between 1949 and 1956, the overwhelming majority unarmed. Meanwhile, Israel enacted the Law of Return which entitles any Jew from anywhere in the world (and now grandchildren of a Jew and their spouses) to "return" to Israel. Israel has always refused to entertain any possibility of a return to Israel for any Palestinian refugees because this would compromise the Jewishness of its state.

The UN estimate of refugees does not take into account a further 250,000 refugees who fled to Jordan when Israel occupied the West Bank in 1967 or who were studying, working or travelling abroad at that time. As the West Bank was administered by Jordan between 1948 and 1967, they were not considered refugees as they still had access to Jordan and were therefore technically displaced within the same territory. They are still refused permission by Israel to return to their homes in the West Bank.

One third of the world's refugees, approximately 3.7 million, are now Palestinian. Many of them live in squalid refugee camps on Israel's borders in Lebanon and Jordan. The diaspora, however, extends around the world. In one respect the fate of the 1948 refugees falls out of the scope of this book. However, their future is integral to the future of the West Bank and any future settlement. If, as the world seems to, one accepts the validity of a state whose requirements for new citizenship is based on racial grounds, then it is clear that the refugees cannot be permitted to return to Israel. The right of return is, however, a personal right and cannot be negotiated away by their leaders. In any case, if a Palestinian leader tried to reach a settlement without incorporating the refugees, he would not be backed by Palestinians as a whole. The refugee problem is not insoluble. In reality, many who have emigrated to the West would not choose to return and would settle for compensation and a right to visit their homeland. It does, however, present a real problem in arriving at any solution.

Girl, Askar Refugee Camp, Nablus

2007

> " They want the land and not the people. It is a silent economic transfer, not like before when they put us on buses. "
>
> **Joseph, Bethlehem**

The concept of transfer has not left Israeli politics. Indeed it is alive and well in the policies implemented by the Israeli government in the West Bank. Again Israel's motivations are largely demographic. It is no longer acceptable internationally to force Palestinians on to buses at gunpoint and deport them. However, Israel has imposed a regime on Palestinians in the West Bank that makes life so difficult that those that can leave, increasingly do so.

The Wall's route has left 47,000 non-Jerusalem-resident Palestinians on the Israeli side. These people live in enclaves, usually surrounded by Israeli settlements, and must apply for temporary permits to remain in their houses. With no rights to access Israel itself, to access medical services and other necessities of life, they must cross to the West Bank using gates in the Wall, the opening hours of which are often restricted with no emergency access. Some Palestinian villages within enclaves have not been connected to water and electricity networks and are forced to depend on tanker deliveries and generators. Meanwhile, on the West Bank side, some Palestinian areas have been almost completed surrounded by the Wall as it ducks back in towards Israel to exclude Palestinian population centres. For example, the Bir Nabala enclave to the north of Jerusalem shown on the map on page 79 now has only one access road. The city of Qalqilya which lies adjacent to the Green Line in the northern West Bank has suffered the same fate but has also been cut off from much of its agricultural lands. Israel is seeking to make life so difficult for the people living in these enclaves that they move further east or leave the West Bank completely. Once sufficient numbers leave, the gaps in access roads can be closed and the Wall straightened to include them within Israel.

The second section of this book sets out the various methods by which Israel is strangling life in the West Bank. They include separation of families, stifling of business, the obstruction of education, restrictions on movement and the use of excessive force. This process is termed the "Quiet Transfer" because of its silent but unrelenting effect. By essentially making the West Bank a big prison Israel intends to reduce the size of the Palestinian population and subdue those who remain. Inevitably it is easier for those with wealth, education or contacts to emigrate, and this loss of talented and influential people is causing great damage to Palestinian society and identity.

The concept of forced transfer is, however, alive and well. It is freely talked of in Israeli political circles and one party, Moledet, is officially committed to the transfer of Palestinians out of Israel. As Israel implements its annexation policy in the West Bank, it is not inconceivable that at some stage Palestinians remaining in annexed areas or Israel itself will be transferred to areas of Palestinian control.

Palestinians waiting to pass
through Tulkarm checkpoint

"In 1948 I was 32 and living on our land near Jaffa [now a suburb of Tel Aviv] when the Haganah attacked us. They began to shoot everywhere, to kidnap children, and to push us off our land. They blocked Jaffa bridge – the main road to supply food and water. Armed groups were everywhere, shooting. Jewish aircraft fired on us. I was hit in the shoulder.

Our cows became weak because of the closures so we left all our animals behind. We fled with just the clothes we were wearing, leaving everything behind. It took us four days to walk in rain to the village of Jaljulia on the Green Line. We were forced to move on to Qalqilya because of lack of food and water and because the Jews were following us. I lost two daughters in Qalqilya because of lack of breast milk and water.

After that we moved to Nablus and lived for three years in caves in the mountains because we were scared of being attacked by the Israelis. Sometimes snow covered the doors of the cave. There were many snakes. I lost three more daughters in this period.

After that we rented a house and spent seven years there before UNRWA [the UN Palestinian refugee support unit] created Askar camp in 1957. We moved to New Askar camp in 1964. I am now 89. Two sons and two daughters have survived."

Sadiqa Issa, refugee, New Askar Refugee Camp

Sadiqa Issa Abu Sarriya, refugee,
New Askar Camp, Nablus

"I met Alex on my birthday when I was in Ramallah. I invited her back to Nablus. She stayed and worked here and after a couple of months we got married. She then went back to England and wasn't allowed to re-enter by the Israelis when she tried to return. I went to meet her in Jordan and we stayed together in a hostel. We couldn't afford an apartment because I could only work illegally and so was badly paid. After eight months we had had enough so I came back to Nablus and she returned to London. We keep in contact by phone but I have no job here, so it's difficult.

I have four friends in Nablus with the same problem. I have instructed a lawyer to take the case to the Israeli Supreme Court. The lawyer asked for 6,000 shekels [US$1,330] up front.

We can't apply for a UK visa until Alex qualifies as a resident again. If I lose the court case, moving to the UK is our last chance but I'm not thinking about that because I want to settle down here.

The Israelis don't want us to breathe here. You can't live without your family so you leave the country."

Mohammed, Balata Refugee Camp

Author's note

Mohammed showed me a letter from the British government stating that they had objected to the practice of refusing entry to international (i.e. non-Palestinian) spouses and that the Israeli government had agreed to stop it. Israel, however, has a history of agreeing to international requests and then ignoring them. Exceptions are made where people have influence, for example where a French woman married to a Palestinian used her contacts with US AID. However, I met a Dominican woman in the same position who was living illegally in the West Bank because she knew her country would have no influence to enable her to return if she leaves Palestine. Approximately 130,000 Palestinians living outside the West Bank are married to West Bank Palestinians and for them the door is closed.

Mohammed, Balata Refugee Camp

Mural on a house in Deheisheh Refugee Camp, Bethlehem. The red rose is a symbol of martyrs who have died for the Palestinian cause while the tents show the conditions refugees were faced with when the camp was established.

3 | Identity

For most of its existence Israel has openly opposed the concept of a Palestinian state. The PLO (the Palestinian Liberation Organization, an umbrella organization internationally acknowledged as the representative body of all Palestinians) first indicated its willingness to accept the right of Israel to exist, and the limitation of Palestinian nationalist aspirations to the Occupied Territories, in 1988 and officially recognized Israel in 1993. However, Israel has consistently declined to recognize Palestinians' right to a viable independent state. With the election of Hamas to the government of the Palestinian Authority, enormous pressure has been applied by the West on Hamas to, amongst other things, recognize Israel. Hamas' refusal to do so does not endear it to western society and is probably a mistake because unofficially Hamas does accept that Israel's existence is a fact which cannot be undone. However, it should be borne in mind that we are asking Hamas to recognize a country that refuses to define its own borders and by implication and by evidence on the ground, considers land which is internationally acknowledged to be Palestinian to be part of its territory.

Zionists and the Israeli state have always challenged Palestinian identity, preferring to identify Palestinians as Arabs. This has the advantage linguistically of dislocating Palestinians from the geographical area of Palestine and allows many Jewish Israelis to believe that Palestinians should, and eventually will, transition to other states, Jordan in particular. Ariel Sharon repeatedly stated that "Jordan is Palestine" in the 1980s. Militarily Israel is secure but, while there remains a Palestinian identity, it cannot exorcise the ghosts of its creation. The history of dispossession of the Palestinians means that Israel cannot be fully legitimized until the Palestinians are either given their own state, accommodated within Israel, or their identity is subsumed within another state. Israel would clearly prefer the latter.

In fact Palestinians have a much more readily identifiable identity than Israeli Jews. Christian and Muslim Palestinians share a common language, culture and history. In contrast, Jewish immigrants to Palestine have often had little in common. Arriving from many points in the diaspora, they had no common language (even Hebrew), had varying religious practices and great cultural differences. As generations of Israelis have been born in Israel an identity has been forged but it is constantly challenged by new arrivals, for example the influx of one million Russians in the 1980s. The IDF has greatly influenced the development of Israeli society, with national service serving to glue the immigrant nation together. However, this bonding is built around at the very least a contempt for Palestinians.

Copy of a Palestinian note issued
during the British mandate

Although Palestinians have a strong historical identity, they only developed nationalist tendencies with the arrival of large numbers of Jews in Palestine. Like most Arab peoples, they see themselves as very distinct from their neighbours. The years of struggle have strengthened this identity within the Occupied Territories and throughout the Palestinian diaspora dispersed around the globe. Within the West Bank, there is a strong desire for a Palestinian state within the 1967 borders. Such a solution is, however, a compromise born out of reality. Of course for most Palestinians living within the West Bank, the territory is their historic home. However, many others are refugees from lands now forming part of Israel. The oldest generation of refugees were born on land now part of Israel and many of them, and their children, understandably dream of returning. However, most do not want to see Israelis driven into the sea. They accept, sometimes reluctantly, that for the increasing number of Israelis born within Israel, Palestine is their home. Many in principle do not object to "sharing" a single state with Jewish Israelis. Palestinians' objection to Israel lies not in its very existence but in the inequalities and injustices that it imposes on them. The overwhelming desire of Palestinians in the West Bank is to be treated fairly, to share Palestine's resources on an equal basis with Israeli Jews.

Israel is not, however, prepared to offer equality. The attitude has always been that Israel is a Jewish state for the benefit of Jews in Israel and around the world. Palestinian citizens (who are seen as a potential threat from within) are tolerated under sufferance and are given inferior rights. Israel has expended great effort to weaken the identity of its one million Palestinian citizens. It has seen this as the way to separate them from other Palestinians outside Israel, further reduce their influence within Israel and perpetuate the inequalities which it sees as essential for the maintenance of the Jewish character of the state. This has largely failed, resulting in increasing demands in Israel for separation of Jews and Arabs, perhaps foreshadowing a forced transfer of Palestinian Israelis to a Palestinian sub-entity.

Israel has applied a similar logic to the West Bank. By dividing the West Bank into enclaves it restricts the flow of national consciousness. By making it difficult to travel, the normal mix of people and ideas which take place within a territory is disrupted. Restrictions on study at university place a brake on institutions which are key to Palestinians' future identity. Confiscation of land deprives families of their historic connection with the soil and creates more urban, itinerant populations. Once land is settled by Israelis, its Palestinian character is destroyed or appropriated as Jewish. By restricting Palestinians' contact with the outside world, Israel limits Palestinians' ability to project their identity. The creation of enclaves has allowed Israel to develop a model of separation akin to apartheid. Israeli settlers can now commute to Israel from deep in the West Bank without any contact with Palestinian life.

Old man leaving the UNWRA
centre at Deheisheh Refugee
Camp, Bethlehem

Part 1: Calibrating to Reality   55

In refugee camps, one frequently sees murals depicting the refugees' heritage, showing pastoral scenes and their villages in Israel that they were forced to leave behind. In some ways Palestinian national identity is stronger in refugee camps, because their desperate conditions mean their need for a solution is more pressing. However, as most of them have spent their whole lives in these cramped, built-up environments, refugees have no real connection with their ancestral lands. Families ensure that the tradition is passed down the generations but in reality it is now solidarity in survival as much as history which binds these communities together. For most Palestinians in camps, their most important possessions are their UN cards recognizing them as refugees. In one sense this is another link to their lands in Israel and evidence of their right to return but more prosaically it entitles them to UN humanitarian support. The pressing need to live will always triumph over dreams and Israel knows this only too well.

Jerusalem and the Palestinian identity

East Jerusalem is central to the Palestinian identity. It is the focal point of the Palestinians' religions and culture. They view East Jerusalem as their future capital. It is something no Palestinian leader can give up.

When Israel occupied the Old City of Jerusalem in 1967, the Israeli authorities demolished many Palestinian houses near the Wailing Wall to allow for the small Jewish presence to be expanded into a Jewish quarter. The Palestinians living there were moved to Shuafat refugee camp on the edge of East Jerusalem and became refugees in their own city. They now face being exiled from Jerusalem itself, as the Wall has been built between them and the City. They have access via a checkpoint at present, but for how long?

Once, almost the whole of the Old City was Palestinian. However, shown the way by Ariel Sharon, Jews have increasingly occupied houses in the Muslim Quarter of the Old City near Damascus Gate, often offering large sums for properties. To date most Palestinians have resisted the temptation. Today, the Muslim Quarter remains the heart of Palestinian life in the Old City. This hold must be maintained if Israel is to be prevented from ultimately judaizing the entire Old City and realizing its objective of making Jerusalem the indivisible capital of Israel.

Orthodox Jew walking through the streets of the Muslim Quarter, Old City, Jerusalem. Increasing numbers of Palestinian houses in the Quarter have been occupied by Jews seeking to judaize the Old City.

"I have been a professional actor and theatre director. I worked as art director at Jerusalem circus, a mixed Israeli and [East Jerusalem] Palestinian group. The circus refused to cross the Wall and perform for Palestinians on the other side. They said, "We don't go to places like that." They refused even to walk to Qalandia checkpoint in solidarity so I resigned and decided to set up the Palestinian Circus School.

This show is for everybody. For most it is the first time they have seen circus. We present all the problems we face as Palestinians – the Wall, checkpoints, challenges to society – but we also want to show people that we want to laugh and that we are not terrorists. We know who are the terrorists.

What is culture? How can it stay alive? Everything is cut up here. As Palestinians we are trying, especially in our centres, to keep the culture of music and the culture of dance. In 2007 we will put on live traditional music and step dance.

We have some sponsors but no fundraising mechanism. Some materials were provided by circuses abroad but I am paying for the performance myself. Now I am unemployed and broke but will never break my work and dream for every Palestinian to see circus."

Shadi, Director of the Palestinian Circus School

Performers of the Palestinian
Circus School in action

Olive tree with bulldozer marks, most probably taken from a Palestinian olive grove, replanted in the middle of a roundabout in Ma'ale Adumim settlement

4 | Resistance and democracy

The Palestinians have never constituted a united, coherent military force. On the two occasions the Palestinians did build up regional power bases they were destroyed, first when the Jordanian government attacked the PLO's guerrilla army in Jordan and expelled it from the country in 1970 and then when Israel forced the PLO into exile in Tunis from its base in Beirut in 1982.

Since 1967, Israel has ruled the Occupied Territories with an iron fist. Two national resistance campaigns have been mounted by the Palestinians during this period. The first *intifada* (literally "shaking off") which took place between 1988 and 1991 was a spontaneous, grassroots movement which developed out of the frustrations Palestinians felt towards continuing occupation. Although resistance was largely restricted to stone throwing and non-violent means, particularly the withholding of taxes, the *intifada* was violently crushed by the IDF.

The second *intifada* was sparked by the provocative visit of Ariel Sharon (then the Israeli opposition leader) to the Haram al-Sharif (Temple Mount) in Jerusalem in September 2000. It saw a change of tactics from the Palestinians, who employed weapons and suicide bombs against the Israelis. The Palestinians' access to weapons was limited but the suicide bomb campaign in particular struck fear into Israelis. Israel's response, as ever, was brutal. Between March and May 2002 Israel reoccupied areas under Palestinian control in the West Bank under Operation Defensive Shield and in this period the UN estimates 497 Palestinians were killed, and 1,447 wounded. The second *intifada* is generally considered to have ceased in 2005 and there is now very little Palestinian violence emanating from the West Bank.

Since 1988, the Palestinian leadership has engaged fully in the various peace processes which the great powers have sponsored. Israel, however, has used the drop in the region's international profile after each process to increase the pace of its colonization of the West Bank. The Palestinians accepted the basis for the last peace process, the Roadmap, unreservedly. In contrast, Israel imposed a host of unreasonable conditions which would have rendered any negotiations pointless, for example no discussion of Israeli settlements or Jerusalem, and no reference to UN Resolution 242. The reality is that Israel does not see a negotiated settlement to be in its interests because it believes it has the ability to dictate events on the ground.

Despite Israel's intransigence, the Palestinian leadership has moved steadily towards a politically-based approach. Even Hamas, which was opposed to the Oslo Accords, has entered the democratic process and maintained long periods of abstention from violence

Entrance to An-Najar University, Nablus

against Israelis despite frequent Israeli assassinations of leading Hamas figures. The two main parties, Fatah and Hamas, still have militant offshoots over which they exercise varying degrees of control. There are also independent groups like Islamic Jihad which are still committed to armed resistance. However, these militant groups have wide support and the power to defend themselves, so they cannot simply be disbanded.

With the full support of the international community, elections were held for a Palestinian legislature in January 2006. They were acknowledged to be free and fair and there was a turnout of 78%. However, the Palestinians did not follow the script. They elected Hamas, on an anti-corruption platform and exposed Western governments' hypocrisy – to them, democracy in the Middle East means electing parties to power which serve the West's interests. As punishment the US and Europe suspended aid to the Palestinian Authority. This has actually strengthened Hamas's support amongst Palestinians. However, democracy without power is of little consequence. As one Palestinian said to me: "Many have arrived at the conclusion that democracy is a joke. It is too subject to external influences and inter-party struggles. The facts on the ground are guns and influence." The world may pay a high price for rejecting democracy in Palestine.

The reality is that the Palestinians' attempts to win independence through violence have failed. Yet violence appears to be the only language that Israel understands. Israel has only ever conceded territory when threatened militarily – withdrawing from Sinai in 1979 following the Camp David Accords, which resulted from an unexpectedly strong military showing by Egypt in the 1973 Yom Kippur War, and from southern Lebanon in 2000 under pressure from Hizbollah. The tragedy for the Palestinians is that they have never had the means or the allies to confront Israel with any chance of success. The campaign of suicide bombing although abhorrent to many Palestinians was perhaps their most successful tactic. However, it ultimately led to the building of the walls which are now imprisoning them. A military option may no longer exist.

And peaceful resistance? Political discourse is not encouraged by Israel. Political protest marches and meetings are restricted to a maximum of ten people. Political articles and pictures cannot be distributed or nationalist songs sung. Indeed, Israel's definition of security is so wide, Palestinians can be arrested for practically any form of public activity. Villagers from Budrus and Beli'een, north of Jerusalem, have employed innovative peaceful protests against the routing of the Wall through their village each Friday for two years as it was being built. It attracted the attention of journalists on the ground and Israeli peace groups, and was well reported within Israel. However, it amounted to just a pebble in the sea of international news. It is an unfortunate fact that in the post 9/11 world, where the US is absorbed by Iraq and the world is getting increasingly used to its daily atrocities, nobody is listening.

Carvings showing the Dome of the Rock and the cartoon figure, Hanthala, a symbol of resistance, made by a Palestinian for his son during his seven years in prison for membership of the PFLP political party

"In the UK you have civilians, but not in Israel. Every Israeli is a soldier and a legitimate target except those under 16 – that would be *haram* [forbidden by God]."

Refugee, Jenin

"I'm against suicide bombings because we shouldn't criticize Israelis and then behave the same as them. Why bomb Israel when we can target tanks on our doorstep?"

Mahmoud, student

"Israel built up Hamas to face up to the nationalists. Who used to support Saddam? The US of course! During the first *intifada* there was no religious element in Gaza. Hamas now supply food and other help so people support them."

Mohammed, Tulkarm

"The Israelis created Hamas to counter Arafat – they backed them with money and weapons. People criticize Arafat but no-one went further than him sitting down at the negotiating table."

Nadim, Taybeh

"All the people are fed up with Fatah. They are like a mafia. They have done nothing for us except steal – steal our land, our money. I am Christian but I give my vote to Hamas – they are all we have. Hamas operations are seen as good when they are in retaliation for assassinations or other Israeli actions but in times of peace Hamas are not thanked for bringing back checkpoints and violence to the West Bank. It is a difficult balance."

Ibrahim, Christian taxi driver, Bethlehem

"We do not vote according to party here but according to the person. If he is a good man we vote for him."

Mohammed, Nahallin

Israeli commuters travelling to work on bus 175 from Ma'ale Adumim settlement to Jerusalem, 8.30 a.m. Wednesday. Since January 2001, 469 Israeli civilians have been killed by Palestinian attacks within Israel, many of them in bus suicide bombings. Hamas justifies each of its attacks by reference to specific Israeli attacks on Palestinians. In recent years Hamas has held strictly to unilateral ceasefires despite frequent Israeli assassinations of leading Hamas figures, attacks which have usually been accompanied by significant loss of life amongst Palestinian civilians.

"My family used to have their own land. A Palestinian spy sold it to the Israelis so I killed him with another man under orders from the PLO. Spies used to go to old men or youngsters and ask for the ownership papers. I was seventeen – I didn't know any better. We sold for a cheap price thinking the land was going to Palestinians. They built the Hefez and Enav settlements. Now the Israelis just take land.

My house was destroyed by the Israelis in 1985 as a punishment. My family – my parents, brothers, sisters, nine altogether – lived for ten years in one room while I was in prison. I didn't have a chance to study in prison, when I was released I didn't have anything to do. Before prison I had dreamed of continuing my studies. My grandfather was a teacher in Saudi Arabia. Now I try to make a living as a farmer. I have no other choice."

Khalid, farmer, Anabta

Khalid and family, Anabta

"I sent my first son to England to study at Bolton University. He was angry at first. He wanted to stay here and fight for his country. But what good would he have been joining the youths with stones, revolvers and Kalashnikovs when they fight against tanks and F16s? It is better to use your mind and help your country that way. Now he agrees."

Mohammed, businessman, Tulkarm

Mohammed and his second son,
Esmat, eating breakfast, Tulkarm

Esmat is a student. He wishes to complete his studies and then study abroad. The faces of martyrs stare out from the walls of his room at home, not because he is a radical but because they were his friends.

Amr was throwing Molotov cocktails at the polluting Israeli chemical factories built on Palestinian land upwind from Tulkarm when he was shot in the leg by an Israeli soldier. His reaction was to obtain a gun from someone in the refugee camp and, with a friend, shoot several settlers living in a nearby settlement.

He knew he would be caught. It was inevitable that someone would inform on him. If the Palestinian Authority got to him first he would be imprisoned. If it was the Israelis, chances are he would be killed. One day his car was targeted by an Israeli missile. He was killed. His friend jumped out in time but was tracked down and killed a few days later.

Ayman was killed planting a bomb at the entrance to Tulkarm refugee camp where Israeli soldiers, his intended target, regularly stand at the entrance and fire into the camp. Esmat knew three others who were killed by the IDF while just standing in the street. As Esmat said, "Staying clean is no protection."

The author

Hanthala has become a symbol of Palestinian identity and defiance. A refugee child, he is always drawn from behind, looking into Palestine from outside. He was conceived by Naji al-Ali, a Palestinian political cartoonist who was assassinated in London in 1987. Mossad, Israel's international intelligence service, was implicated in the killing and Britain expelled two Israeli diplomats and closed Mossad's offices in London as a result.

PART 2:

LIFE

5 | The conquest of Jerusalem

Under international law the Green Line, separating Israel from the territories it occupied in the West Bank in 1967, divides Israeli West Jerusalem and Palestinian East Jerusalem. Palestinians see East Jerusalem as their future capital and in international diplomatic circles Tel Aviv and not Jerusalem is viewed as Israel's capital. However, Israel effectively annexed East Jerusalem in 1967 by extending the city's municipal boundaries the day following its occupation and formally did so in 1980 when it declared Jerusalem as its united and indivisible capital.

Logic and fairness dictate that in any future settlement, Palestinian East Jerusalem should be governed by Palestinians and that the Old City should become an international city governed for the benefit of Jews, Christians and Muslims alike. Indeed, Jerusalem was designated an international city in the original 1947 partition plan. On the Haram al-Sharif (Temple Mount) are built the Dome of the Rock and Al-Aqsa mosques, the latter the third most holy mosque in Islam. Muslims believe Mohamed ascended to heaven from here and consider it to be the closest place to heaven on earth. For Christians, it is the city where Jesus was crucified and resurrected. For Jews it is the site of the First and Second Temples and the central point of their faith. To the Israeli state, however, this shared reverence is of no relevance – Jerusalem is a Jewish city.

Everything about Israeli policy towards Jerusalem works towards the city's judaization. The state and the Jerusalem municipality act like a landlord agitating for the surrender of a tenant's lease. Despite the annexation and incorporation of East Jerusalem into the municipality, its Palestinian citizens only have resident status. Although this gives them permission to continue to live in East Jerusalem and claim health and certain other benefits from the Israeli state, it is a temporary status which is open to cancellation in the future. Since 1995, if a Palestinian with residency leaves Jerusalem and acquires residency or nationality in any other country, or is simply unable to prove his or her "centre of life" is within the city, his or her Jerusalem residency is liable to be cancelled, resulting in denial of access to the city of his or her birth. Between 1996 and 2000, 2,200 ID cards were cancelled, forcing 8,800 Palestinians to leave the city.

The Wall resembles a snake, deviating from the municipal boundary to maximize the number of Israeli settlements and Palestinian open land on the Jerusalem side and minimize the number of Palestinians. This can be clearly seen on the map [opposite] where the Wall loops around Shuafat refugee camp, leaving its 30,000 Palestinian inhabitants on the West Bank side. It does not take a fortune teller to predict that at some time in the future the municipal boundary will be adjusted to the line of the Wall,

Central West Bank Barrier
| RAMALLAH | JERUSALEM | NORTH BETHLEHEM |

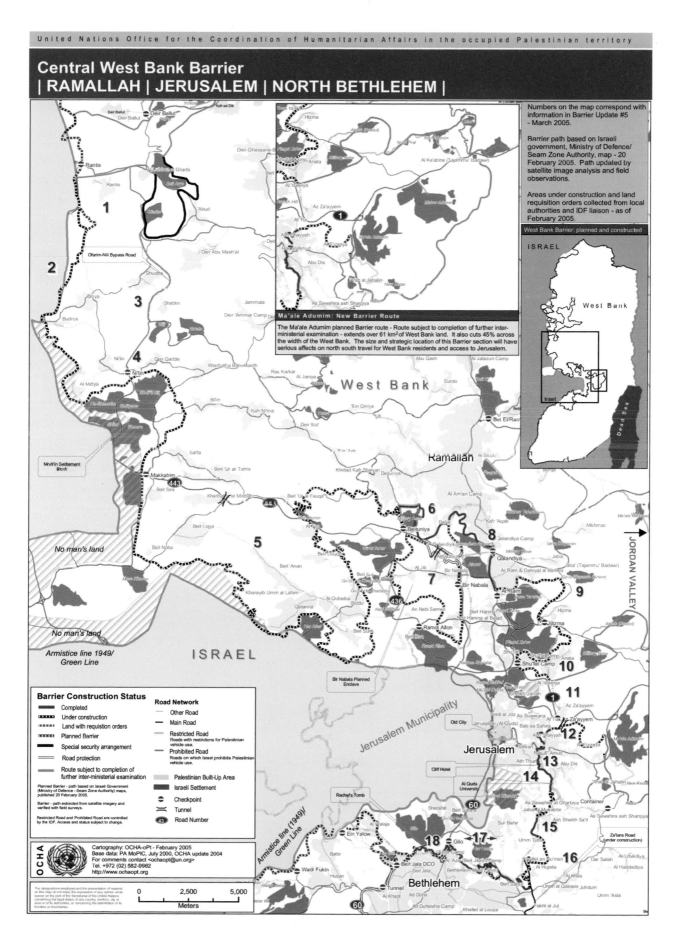

Numbers on the map correspond with information in Barrier Update #5 - March 2005.

Barrier path based on Israeli government, Ministry of Defence/ Seam Zone Authority, map - 20 February 2005. Path updated by satellite image analysis and field observations.

Areas under construction and land requisition orders collected from local authorities and IDF liaison - as of February 2005.

West Bank Barrier: planned and constructed

Ma'ale Adumim: New Barrier Route

The Ma'ale Adumim planned Barrier route - Route subject to completion of further inter-ministerial examination - extends over 61 km² of West Bank land. It also cuts 45% across the width of the West Bank. The size and strategic location of this Barrier section will have serious affects on north south travel for West Bank residents and access to Jerusalem.

Barrier Construction Status
- Completed
- Under construction
- Land with requisition orders
- Planned Barrier
- Special security arrangement
- Road protection
- Route subject to completion of further inter-ministerial examination

Planned Barrier - path based on Israeli Government (Ministry of Defence - Seam Zone Authority) maps, published 20 February 2005.

Barrier - path extracted from satellite imagery and verified with field surveys.

Restricted Road and Prohibited Road are controlled by the IOF. Access and status subject to change.

Road Network
- Other Road
- Main Road
- Restricted Road — Roads with restrictions for Palestinian vehicle use.
- Prohibited Road — Roads on which Israel prohibits Palestinian vehicle use.
- Palestinian Built-Up Area
- Israeli Settlement
- Checkpoint
- Tunnel
- Road Number

Cartography: OCHA-oPt - February 2005
Base data: PA MoPIC, July 2000, OCHA update 2004
For comments contact <ochaopt@un.org>
Tel. +972 (02) 582-9962
http://www.ochaopt.org

The designations employed and the presentation of material on this map do not imply the expression of any opinion whatsoever on the part of the Secretariat of the United Nations concerning the legal status of any country, territory, city or area or of its authorities, or concerning the delimitation of its frontiers or boundaries.

0   2,500   5,000
Meters

leaving Palestinians with Jerusalem residency status exposed. However, Israel's decision to retain most of East Jerusalem behind the Wall rather than to route the Wall according to security concerns (along the Green Line) has left 230,000 East Jerusalem Palestinians on the Israeli side.

Israel is trying to separate the Palestinian populations in East Jerusalem and the rest of the West Bank. It hopes by forcing separation, it will cause Palestinians to depopulate Jerusalem or, if that fails, at least to reduce them to a state of passivity. It does not want them to be subject to nationalist influences from over the Wall. Consequently it is illegal for Jerusalem ID holders to enter towns under Palestinian control. Under a law brought in in January 2007, it is illegal for a West Bank ID holder to travel in the car of a Jerusalem ID holder without a permit, even if they are related. West Bank Palestinians can only travel to East Jerusalem with an Israeli permit, granted in diminishing numbers and increasingly only for special occasions like Christmas. This example of the Quiet Transfer policy has, however, actually resulted in many Palestinians with the right of residency moving back into the city from the West Bank, and putting up with overcrowded conditions in order to protect their status and access to jobs, hospitals and schools.

Israel has populated East Jerusalem with approximately 180,000 settlers. Many of the remaining 260,000 settlers in the West Bank live in settlements surrounding East Jerusalem. The Israeli strategy is clear – to isolate Palestinian East Jerusalem by surrounding it with Jewish settlements, thereby preventing any possibility of East Jerusalem becoming a Palestinian capital in the future. The construction of the Wall surrounding these new settlements is one step in completing this process. The final piece is the construction of settlements on the area of land known as E1 – which Israel has so far resisted due to international pressure. While the E1 area remains open land, the Palestinians still have potential for a contiguous state incorporating East Jerusalem. Israel has though recently proposed a settlement corridor in this area consisting of 3,500 housing units and commercial and industrial zones.

It should be remembered that under international law East Jerusalem and the West Bank form part of a single territory. Historically the Palestinian towns and villages to the north, south and east of East Jerusalem have looked to it as a centre for employment, trade, religion and social activities. These contacts used to account for between 30 and 40% of Palestinian GDP. Palestinians in Jerusalem are being separated from their relatives, friends and countrymen in the West Bank by the Wall. Businesses and customers are split. Israeli authorities have tried to confiscate property within Jerusalem belonging to West Bank residents under absentee landlord legislation and although the Israeli courts have declared such action illegal it may only be a matter of time before the law is validated by the government.

Tea seller touts for business
after nightfall during Ramadan,
a month of fasting in the daytime
and celebration in the evening,
Damascus Gate, Jerusalem

A 1991 report revealed that Palestinians made up 28% of Jerusalem's population but received between 2 and 12% of the municipal budget despite being subject to a common tax regime. The lack of equality can be seen by a simple visual comparison of the streets of East and West Jerusalem. Palestinians suffer from inadequate roads, lighting, sewers and refuse collection while lacking public parks, sporting facilities, and educational and cultural centres. On 19 April 1999 an inter-ministerial committee on Jerusalem advised that, in order to maintain a 70/30 Jewish majority in Jerusalem, Israel needed to build 116,000 new housing units for Jews by 2020. Since 1967, 35% of the land in East Jerusalem has been expropriated for the construction of Jewish neighbourhoods containing 47,000 new housing units. In addition 54% of land has been designated as security areas, "green areas", or Jewish residential zones from which Palestinians are excluded. Only about 5% of building permit applications applied for by Palestinians are approved.

Jerusalem should be an example to the world. It could be a prosperous and vibrant city, the capital of two peoples living side by side in an atmosphere of tolerance and liberalism. Instead Israel is determined to complete its judaization. The western world is preoccupied with Iraq but it would be a mistake to believe the Muslim world has been sidetracked to the same extent. Christian leaders seem prepared to stand by while their faith is levered out of the Holy Land but it is unlikely that Muslims will be so compliant. This will have consequences for us all.

Boy from Shuafat refugee camp flying a kite over land where the Wall now stands, separating the camp on the right from land and settlements in Jerusalem on the left. The Wall follows the dirt track running from the left up the centre of the picture.

"How do Israelis acquire land in East Jerusalem? There are lots of cases of forged papers or of someone who is not the owner selling. Most land in East Jerusalem is unregistered so proving ownership can be difficult. There is one case at the moment along the line of the Wall where a hotel lies within the Municipality but its owners live outside East Jerusalem which the Israelis are trying to confiscate.

There is a village called Nabi Samuel which has existed since before 1948 but is not recognized by Israel. It is 200 metres from a settlement. The villagers have tried several times to build a two- or three-room school and each time it has been knocked down. The Israeli authorities get to know if anybody adds a room, builds a balcony or shelter for sheep without permission and ensure demolition.

They cut people off from their land. They take ID cards away. Where else in the world would people born in their homeland only be considered residents and be liable to lose status at any moment.

If a Palestinian lives for seven years (sometimes less) outside the city or gets any residency or passport of another country, he immediately loses his residency rights. I have dozens of these cases. They cancel the ID numbers from the computer and then they can come back only as tourists. They are basically deleting the history of our people and the city.

Not everybody has the money, the courage, the guts to fight the state. Most people say "what can I do?", leave and never come back.

There is a new law which applies only to Palestinians. It says Palestinians can only apply for family reunion if the woman is over 25 and the man over 35. This is very problematic in our society where people marry early. One of the twelve [Israeli] Supreme Court judges was brave enough to tell the truth – she said it was not about security but demography.

There are 130,000 Palestinians from the West Bank who are married to Palestinians outside the West Bank, particularly Jordan, whose cases are frozen. The door is totally shut. I know a man who travels from Nablus to Amman every week or two to see his family."

Muhammad Dahleh, Lawyer, Jerusalem

Muhammad Dahleh, Lawyer,
Jerusalem

"The Bustan [an area of Silwan, an East Jerusalem suburb] has 88 houses and 1,500 people. A year ago they all received [Israeli] demolition orders as illegal buildings but all these buildings are "illegal" [in their eyes]. They include an extended 18th-century house. The Israelis use any excuse. They want to make it an archeological park. King David was supposed to have gone down there from the temple to pick fruit. They are trying to find ways to get us out of Jerusalem, to persuade us to find a good place elsewhere.

We pay our taxes like anyone in Israel but there are 40,000 people in Silwan and not one playground. We want to use computers and swim with our children like any other people.

On the ground we are losing – they have the money, the power – we can't stop them. Fifty houses have been bought by settlers – not normal people who say hello and goodbye – people with blood in their eyes. They always have guns with a finger on the trigger. The other half of the Israelis don't know we are here – they hear nothing about us on TV – they say [with surprise] "Those are Arab houses?"

They are pressurizing us a lot and when you do that we explode. I was in prison for nine years and practised a lot of violence in the street. I see now that doesn't work but the Israelis don't. We are challenging the municipality in the Israeli courts. People now can't find the money to live. They are just concerned about finding food for their family.

It is difficult. I want my state but I want to be able to go to Jaffa [a suburb of Tel Aviv, which was once a large Palestinian city before the creation of Israel] without crossing borders. But we want to rule ourselves – we can do that successfully."

Abdul, Silwan

Boys in a Silwan street,
East Jerusalem

"I am married to a woman from Hebron. We have four children. They have Jerusalem ID but she hasn't. We married seven years ago and an application for Jerusalem ID for her has been outstanding ever since. She lives illegally with me. When we leave the house she doesn't take her ID card out and says she has forgotten it. Once the wall is finished she won't be able to go back and see her family. If she is discovered she will be sent back across the Wall or maybe to prison."

Abdullah, Jerusalem

Author's note

Since the interview, Abdullah's wife has been granted a temporary permit to stay in Jerusalem with Abdullah and their children. Abdullah is over 35. Under Israeli law, Palestinian men under 35 are not entitled to make applications for family reunification.

Abdullah looking at a picture
of his wife, Jerusalem

"30% of Palestinian shopkeepers in the Old City live over the Wall [on the West Bank side] and will lose their businesses. Another 10% will also leave. That's what the Israelis want. They tell tourists it's dangerous here and keep them in the new city. I pay the same rates as them but my streets are dirty and theirs are clean.

I hope the Wall will be finished soon because we can't stand it much longer. Then there could be peace. One side has to win before there can be peace. But even if they win they don't want peace. They don't want to give back the land they occupied in 1967, or to let Palestinians have their own state. So there will be war."

Shopkeeper, Old City, Jerusalem

Coffee house in the Muslim
Quarter of the Old City, Jerusalem

Har Homa settlement, still undergoing construction, taken from Bethlehem. Prior to 1995 it was a tree-covered hill with the Arabic name Abu Ghuneim. It was confiscated by the Israeli government and although the matter was disputed twice at the UN Security Council in 1995, the US vetoed the resolution both times.

Har Homa is one of the ring of settlements built by the Israelis between East Jerusalem and the rest of the West Bank to effectively ensure the annexation of East Jerusalem to Israel. Its transformation from forest to settlement can be seen in full in a series of photographs at www.arij.org/.

What Did We Do To Deserve This?

Israeli settlers noisily celebrating Hanukkah in a street opposite a Palestinian tourist shop, in the Muslim Quarter of the Old City in East Jerusalem, while a soldier protects them. Settlers have taken over a number of buildings in the Quarter.

6 | **Restrictions on movement**

Israel has established an illegal permit system to control Palestinian movement, which is policed using a highly restrictive network of checkpoints. This breaches Palestinians' right to freedom of movement under international law. West Bank Palestinians are divided into two categories – those who have resident status in East Jerusalem who have blue IDs, and those who do not who have a green ID ("West Bank ID"). Palestinians holding West Bank ID cannot cross the Wall into East Jerusalem without a permit, which must be applied for in advance for a fee. Applications for permits are usually refused. Whereas Israelis universally cross by car, West Bank Palestinians must pass through airport-level security on foot when entering East Jerusalem.

Those to the east of the Wall with land on the Israeli side are losing their livelihoods. 60% of such families are denied access to their land. The older generation who usually own the land are unable to gain access for younger Palestinians to help them cultivate it. Those lucky enough to get permits often find gates closed. Seasonal gates allow access for picking but not ploughing, spraying and pruning, resulting in reduced yields. Fields which were once within walking distance now require long detours to reach. 22% of such land is now only accessible through pedestrian gates. The 47,000 Palestinians without Jerusalem ID located between the Wall and the Green Line require permits, issued on a temporary basis, to stay in their homes. Where residents have not been issued with permits they cannot cross to the rest of the West Bank and access essential services without risking not being allowed to return.

Palestinians also require permits to move within the West Bank. The bureaucratic procedure involved, cost and high chance of refusal work to inhibit movement. West Bank ID holders are not permitted to enter the Jordan Valley without a permit. This creates an invisible wall designed to separate the population of the Jordan Valley, which Israel intends to annex, from the rest of the West Bank. Israel has split the rest of the West Bank into sections and makes it hard for Palestinians to move from one to another. The city of Nablus is surrounded by particularly constrictive checkpoints and Palestinian males between 16 and 30 years old from Nablus and the northern governorates are not permitted to travel to the rest of the West Bank without a permit. Similar restrictions apply to residents in other West Bank towns, for example Bethlehem. Nablus itself, with its 216,000 citizens, is surrounded by six manned checkpoints and two roadblocks.

As of 20 September 2006, there were 528 checkpoints and physical obstacles in the West Bank. This represents almost a 40% increase in the number of physical obstacles since August 2005. Some are manned permanently, some intermittently, while other flying

Israeli police stop all
Palestinians passing by to check
their papers, while an Orthodox
Jew walks on, Jerusalem

checkpoints appear unexpectedly, often at peak travel times severely disrupting Palestinian movement. The West Bank is a small territory totalling 3,000 square miles, 95 miles tall and 35 miles wide. However, checkpoints make even the shortest journey unpredictable. Palestinians often face hours waiting to pass through checkpoints which the Israelis may close at will. A journey from Ramallah to Bethlehem which used to take 35 minutes can take anything between one and six hours because of checkpoints and the requirement to use a precipitous minor road. The original main road is just one of 450 miles of Palestinian roads confiscated for Israeli use. Palestinians are often forced to take long detours to reach destinations which are much closer as the crow flies. Where Palestinians are permitted access to main roads, they are forced to wait at checkpoints while cars with Israeli plates drive through unhindered. Ramallah is only 29 miles from Nablus but Palestinians must pass through three permanent checkpoints to make the journey.

Checkpoints and barriers restrict Palestinians' access to their land, make the transaction of business costly, prevent the sale of agricultural products beyond local markets, make access to universities and medical care more difficult and inhibit social and cultural activities. They are also designed to stagnate Palestinian life – to deter Palestinians from travelling from one area to another, thereby promoting fragmentation of the West Bank, to inhibit the development of Palestinian businesses and agriculture and generally to help persuade Palestinians to leave the West Bank for foreign countries. They are also the one point that ordinary Palestinians encounter Israeli soldiers on a regular, often daily, basis. Such contacts present only danger to Palestinians. They know that an Israeli soldier is unlikely to be reprimanded for any injury they may cause to Palestinians and that the IDF has the power to place them in administrative detention, indefinite imprisonment without charge or trial, if it so chooses. The IDF states that the checkpoints which restrict Palestinian movement are necessary to enable settler freedom of movement, a clear demonstration of Israel's apartheid policy. They also serve as a highly visible demonstration of Israel's control over the West Bank – to show Palestinians on a daily basis that any resistance would be futile.

As one approaches a checkpoint in a Palestinian taxi the tension is palpable. When the taxi reaches the front of the queue, the taxi driver drives tentatively towards the checkpoint and passes the passengers' IDs and permits to the soldier. Heads are down, hands clasped and there is stony silence. If the taxi is pulled over for inspection the mood darkens. As the IDs are returned and the taxi drives off the mood slowly lightens. These are people who face checkpoints whenever they travel, perhaps several in a day. The fear is not of unfamiliarity, of the unusual – it is the fear of everyday reality.

It is difficult to imagine the extent of the checkpoint infrastructure within such a small area. With checkpoints frequently come watchtowers and army bases. Temporary

Watchtower at Gilo checkpoint prior to the building of a new, border crossing-style facility

checkpoints are often more rudimentary, with the road narrowed by concrete blocks or barriers. I have included several photographs of checkpoints and Israeli soldiers manning them but they do not give any idea of their number and density. However, I travelled primarily by Palestinian shared taxi and taking pictures of checkpoints (which are military facilities) is prohibited. For the well-being of my fellow passengers and to reduce the risk of my film being confiscated, I took the minimum I thought necessary

Israel has also imposed border restrictions which limit West Bank Palestinians' ability to travel. As in Jerusalem, if West Bank ID holders are deemed to have moved their "centre of life" away from the West Bank, they are liable to lose their rights to residency there. The test is not related to time but in practice even an absence of 4 years has been judged sufficient. Increasingly, husbands and wives of foreign nationality are denied entry visas to Palestine, forcing families to live apart or the Palestinian partner to leave the West Bank. As Israel has declared the West Bank a closed area, former residents must obtain a permit from the military governor to visit their relatives in the West Bank. This may be refused on any grounds. The tightening of entry policy has resulted in Palestinians overstaying their visas for fear of being refused entry the next time, condemning them to a static life, unable to travel beyond the next checkpoint. Residents of Gaza cannot visit the West Bank although under international law they are a single entity. Israel has refused to negotiate about the building of a corridor between the two entities allowing travel between the two, despite previous commitments to do so.

Dirt road on the way to Taybeh.
Israel has prohibited Palestinians
from using the direct road from
Ramallah to Taybeh so settlers can
have exclusive use of it.
Palestinians must use back roads
which take much longer.

This photograph was taken at a checkpoint while I was travelling from Qalqilya to Ramallah in a minibus. As is normal, the Palestinians handed their ID cards and my passport to the driver to show to the Israeli soldier. The soldier called out the name of the Palestinian man sitting next to me and ordered him to get off the bus. As he left the bus you could sense how fearful he was. The soldier questioned the man aggressively.

The other travellers were clearly concerned. We were ordered to drive forward. After ten minutes the man was allowed to rejoin us. Visibly relieved, the man explained to me that he had all the right papers to travel to Ramallah. Indeed he worked for an Israeli telecoms company, had a pass to travel to Jerusalem and had even travelled to Europe on business with his company. The problem was that he was from the city of Tulkarm and the Israelis had closed Tulkarm that day. "I don't know why but I feel very tired every time I come to Ramallah," he said.

On another day I was travelling from Tulkarm to Qalqilya with a Palestinian friend. At the main checkpoint outside Tulkarm a soldier ordered everybody to get out of the minibus. He examined the Palestinians' ID cards and my passport before handing me back my passport. He then shuffled the ID cards and pulled out one at random which happened to belong to my friend. We were ordered to get back into the bus while my friend was kept back. I was not sure whether identifying myself with him would be a help or a hindrance but I was urged by my fellow travellers to do so. I stood my ground for a while with the soldier but I did not get anywhere and we were forced to leave my friend behind. I called him later and he said that the soldiers had told him that he wouldn't be allowed through the checkpoint that day and would have to come back tomorrow. They gave no reason.

The author

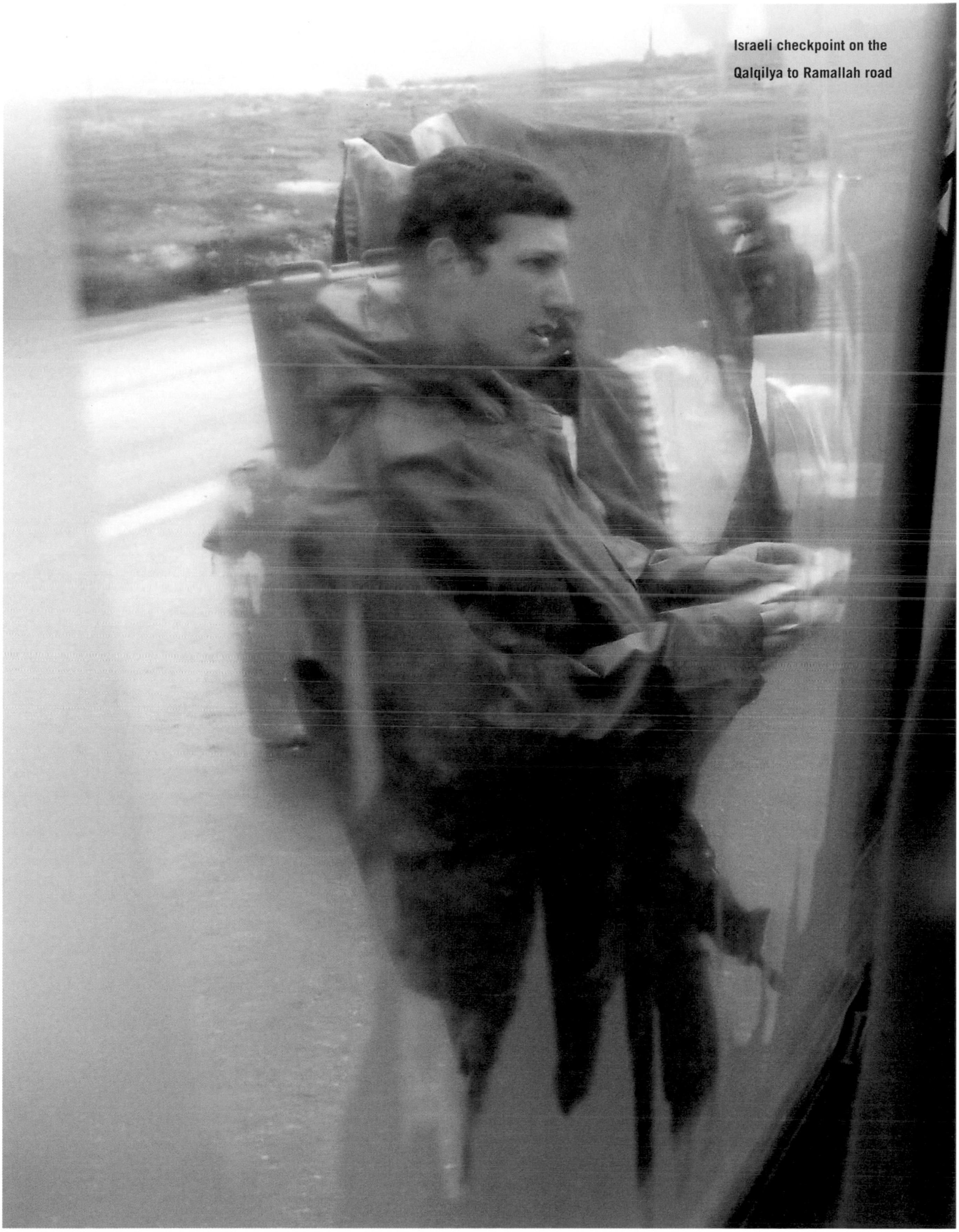

Israeli checkpoint on the Qalqilya to Ramallah road

"I was heavily pregnant with a girl when I developed complications. My doctor advised me to go to hospital as soon as possible. The Israeli soldiers at the checkpoint refused to let me through despite the seriousness of the situation. They pointed guns at my husband, hit him and swore at him. We went to another checkpoint and were refused there so we went home. When we returned, a soldier said: "You've come again. I'm bored with you. I want to kill you and your baby in your stomach." After five hours, they finally let me through and I had to walk for a kilometre before I could find transport. I lost my daughter. I had been trying for a girl for 12 years."

Umm Akram, from a village near Ramallah

Umm Akram, from a village
near Ramallah

"In the past it might take six hours to get from street to street. It is much better now. Israeli soldiers used to shoot at us, jail us, but not now.

This morning we had what should have been a ten minute journey to Daras village. We were stopped at Kefriyat checkpoint for half an hour but a taxi was allowed straight through. I don't know why they are doing this – this is an ambulance for a patient. It was a case of epilepsy; the family were very distressed as they did not know the patient had the condition.

We have to go on long indirect routes – we are not allowed to use Israeli-only roads.

In our job we do not distinguish between Palestinians and Israelis. I do not ask "Are you Jewish?" We are here to help all the people."

Tulkarm ambulance driver

Ambulance at Huwwara

checkpoint near Nablus

Queue of traffic waiting to get
through Tulkarm checkpoint

7 | The Israeli military machine

The Israeli Defence Force (IDF) was founded on 14 May 1948 on the declaration of independence of Israel. As an army it proved itself highly effective in the Arab-Israeli wars. However, with regard to the Palestinians, it has assumed the role of ethnic cleanser, policeman, jailer and executioner. From its very inception the IDF committed massacres of Palestinians in the execution of David Ben Gurion's ethnic cleansing policy. In 1947 Ben Gurion had instituted a "system of aggressive defence; with every Arab attack we must respond with a decisive blow; the destruction of the place or the expulsion of the residents along with the seizure of the place." This principle of using overwhelming and disproportionate force is the true ideology of the IDF and it has been applied consistently down the years, for example in the attacks on Lebanon in August 2006, and in response to Palestinian militant actions, where it finds its expression in military incursions, closures and acts of collective punishment such as house demolitions.

Between 1967 and 1988 the West Bank presented few problems for Israel. However, the outbreak of the first *intifada* in 1988 brought a dramatic change with the deployment of 180,000 troops. For a period after the Oslo Accords intervention was scaled back in Palestinian-controlled areas but the outbreak of the second *intifada* in 2000 brought with it a massive crackdown, known as Operation Defensive Shield, amounting to a re-conquest of these areas.

Over 4,000 Palestinians, most of them unarmed civilians have been killed by Israeli forces since 2000. There is, of course, a threat. In the same period Palestinian armed groups have killed some 700 Israelis in suicide bombs and other attacks. However, Amnesty International describes "a pattern of reckless, disproportionate and excessive use of lethal force by Israeli soldiers". The IDF's rules of engagement permit use of firearms to enforce curfews and against stone throwers. The IDF carries out extrajudicial executions of wanted Palestinians as a substitute for arrest and prosecution. This is itself illegal under international law but such "targeted killings" kill and also wound many innocent people nearby, violating the requirement for it to act proportionally. Israeli authorities routinely fail to investigate allegations of unlawful killings and other abuses of Palestinians by the IDF and settlers. For most Palestinians though, their personal experience of the IDF in their daily lives as they pass through checkpoints is one of random physical abuse, verbal insults, deliberate delays and degrading treatment.

There are currently approximately 8,000 Palestinians detained within Israel prisons, the vast majority for "security offences". Over 2,000 have still to face trial. As of January 2007, 807 Palestinians were being held in "administrative detention", a procedure under

Cry for help, Ramallah

which detainees are held without charge and usually with no intention of bringing the detainees to trial. Administrative detention orders are issued by Israeli army commanders for terms of up to six months and can be renewed indefinitely. In 2006, Israel detained 27 parliamentarians and six ministers. Since 1967 over 650,000 Palestinians have been detained by the Israeli authorities, equating to 40% of the total male Palestinian population in the West Bank and Gaza.

Torture was routinely used by the IDF until it was declared illegal by the Israeli Supreme Court in 2001, despite Israel being a signatory to the UN Convention Against Torture. Now the IDF primarily uses collaborators and surveillance to obtain information from prisoners. Instances of torture are, however, still reported by Palestinian detainees. The Israeli Supreme Court has tempered the excesses of the military on occasion. However, this has tended to be the exception rather than the rule and its actions are usually limited to procedural modifications. Its primary role has been to legitimize the military's actions in the Occupied Territories and to manipulate the legal landscape to achieve this end. For example, it accepts (with selective interpretation) the Hague Regulations which it uses as a basis to justify many of the military's actions but rejects the Fourth Geneva Convention which would impose unwanted restrictions on the management of occupation. In effect, the Court has established a mechanism that permits Israel's continued colonial exploitation of resources and markets and settlement of land.

Many of Israel's leaders have graduated from the IDF's ranks. Menachim Begin led the terrorist movement Irgun which was incorporated within the Israeli army in 1948 and Yitzhak Rabin was second in command of one of the IDF's ethnic cleansing units in the 1948 War. Ariel Sharon was the last Israeli leader to have served at a high rank in the IDF and again, his service record makes grim reading. It was natural for these leaders to use the IDF, in whose ranks they were held in high esteem, as an enforcement mechanism.

The Israeli military is, however, much more than a tool of the Israeli government. The IDF's expansive role and its structured command has provided a steadying influence within the fractured world of Israeli politics and has given its senior officers great influence. With Ariel Sharon's departure from politics following a stroke, the 1948 generation of military leaders has passed into history leaving the armed forces without a respected ex-military leader to keep them in check. Increasingly influenced by its settler contingent, the IDF proceeds apace with land confiscations in the West Bank. It seeks to perpetuate the conflict, provoking Palestinian responses when peace threatens to break out, thereby creating a cycle of violence which reinforces its role. The IDF's history, combined with the machinery of occupation which it has been allowed to build up, presents a great obstacle to change.

Opposite

Abu Ali Mustafa, Secretary General of the Popular Liberation Front of Palestine. He was assassinated by two rockets fired from an Israeli helicopter as he sat at his desk in Ramallah on 27 August 2001.

"All people living in refugee camps live in difficult conditions, not just Jenin. Between 1994 and 2000 life was very difficult. Settlements increased, living standards were low. From 2000 when Sharon entered Al-Aqsa, demonstrations took place in Jalama village near Jenin where the Israelis are based. Every day Israelis were shooting two to three youngsters 10, 15, 18 years old. They were just throwing stones ... nothing. Before 2001 there were no guns or bombs. The Israelis entered the camp seven times before the big attack on Jenin in April 2002 for no reason except the stone throwing. More than 100 were killed, 50 to 60 at Jalama.

The attack lasted fourteen or fifteen days – F16s, Apaches – night and day. 58 died. 150 plus were injured. 2,000 plus were taken to prison. Most are now back – 150 or so remain. Israelis think all refugees, especially in Jenin, are terrorists. They even take 60 year olds. After killing two of my brothers, they took me and four remaining brothers to prison. Our house was destroyed by the Israelis. My brothers – Amjad (30), Mohammed (21) – were fighting for the camp. It was self-defence.

The Israelis came into the camp last week and asked for someone by loudspeaker. Some have guns, some don't – the Israelis kill them anyway. They get their information from spies, by offering women and money, and surveillance in prison – but also by listening in on mobiles and taking pictures from planes.

I have built a house outside the camp. I left the camp for my children. I don't forget my village for my father. In the future we will return to our lands in Israel. This is our right, our fathers' right, our grandfathers' right."

Taisir, a refugee, Jenin

Taisir holding pictures of his
brothers, killed defending Jenin
refugee camp in 2002, Jenin

"Tulkarm refugee camp was constructed in 1948. 148 dunums [36 acres] hold 16,500 people. 23,000 more have left the camp to go to central Tulkarm and other areas around. There are 42 big families from all around Palestine – Haifa, Jaffa, Netanya, Beer Sheba [all now in Israel] and Gaza. Living conditions are very difficult. Sons working in the Gulf and other countries support their families in the camps.

Lack of space causes many social problems. Kids have nowhere to play except the street. They play soldiers all the time – Israelis against Palestinians. A child knows as much as a British soldier about weapons.

The Israelis enter the camp every night. The special forces were here today hunting for somebody. In April 2004 a tank fired at my surgery. I've had to replace the glass five times. Soldiers just fire as they pass. One time three people were killed outside."

Fadi, dentist, Tulkarm refugee camp

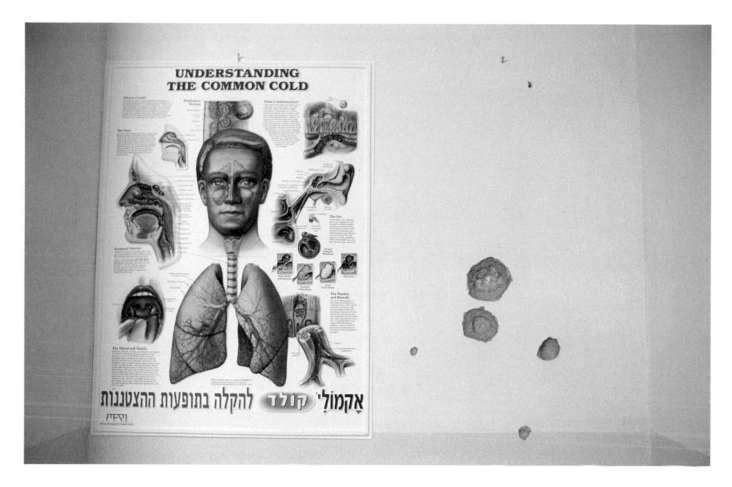

Children entering Fadi's dental surgery through the bullet-riddled door, and shell holes on the waiting room wall, Tulkarm refugee camp

Painting of the Dome of the Rock on a wall in Nablus prison, now a ruin following an Israeli attack. The painting has been sprayed with bullets from a passing Israeli vehicle.

"Nablus has always been the centre of Palestinian politics, commerce and studies. Political movements start here – Arafat came here for six months when he wanted to start Fatah to connect with people. The first *intifada* technically started in Gaza but within six hours it started here. Israelis see Nablus as a balancing point. Problems start here.

You can go home, to work, walk the streets but it is like being in a big prison. We cannot travel easily out of Nablus. The Israelis come in every night. In the day, only one or two hours – quick in and out. At night, they stay all night. They search houses and take six to eight people each night. They depend on informers. They turn the less intelligent and weaker ones in prison by threatening their families. You wake up and know they've been and wonder who is gone.

Some are involved and might take the odd shot but generally they [Palestinian militants] don't confront the Israelis as they know they don't have the military capacity. When Israelis kill people they don't care whether they are active or not. They need to justify to their people that Nablus is a terrorist city."

Client in a Nablus barber shop

Square in the Old City, Nablus

In January 2007 I visited New Askar refugee camp to obtain permission to use an interview and photographs that I had taken of a refugee on a previous visit. While there, I heard that a boy had been killed by the IDF two weeks earlier. Jamil, 14, was playing with a couple of friends in an olive grove adjacent to the camp and next to a road dug into a cutting. It was about midday. The boys told me an IDF vehicle came down the road from a nearby settlement. They looked over the edge of the cutting and a soldier opened fire. Jamil was killed by a bullet to the head. We went to the scene accompanied by Jamil's cousin and I took the photo opposite. Suddenly there was the sound of a vehicle on the road below. Instinctively we all moved away. The cousin said, "It is dangerous here. We should go."

Several days later I visited the camp again to obtain another permission, this time from a refugee called Abdul (see p.170). Abdul greeted me and we sat down with a neighbour who acted as translator. The translator said, "You know one of Abdul's sons was killed a fortnight ago?" I replied "Jamil? Yes, but I didn't know he was Abdul's son." I asked the translator to say I was very sorry. He waved his hand, shrugged his shoulders and said, "Don't worry. This is normal here."

The author

Jamil's martyr poster

What Did We Do To Deserve This?

Jamil's friends standing beside a
memorial to him and looking up at
the Elon Moreh settlement, on the
hill in the distance, from which the
IDF jeep came

"It is good for a Palestinian to spend some time in prison. Those driving cars and listening to radios in Ramallah are not real Palestinians but in prison you meet them – people who will be there for 20 to 30 years for defending their country. My Dad said you need to be in the army or a prison to be a man. I have been in prison so, like my father, I am a man.**"**

Saleh, student

Author's note

Saleh, aged 19, spent four months in an Israeli prison built in the West Bank. Some kids had been throwing stones at Israeli soldiers. They escaped but Saleh, who was unaware of these events, was arrested instead. Two Israeli soldiers testified against him. If he had maintained his innocence he would have been imprisoned for a year or more. He pleaded guilty for the sake of his mother.

Saleh, a student, looking down on the Israeli prison (built on Palestinian farmland) in which he spent four months

Ayda camp, one of three refugee camps in Bethlehem, lies on the north-west edge of the town adjacent to fields of olive trees. In line with its policy to maximize the amount of Palestinian land on the Israeli side of the Wall and minimize the number of Palestinians, Israel has routed the Wall between the olive grove and the camp, leaving only an access road between the Wall and the camp for Palestinians to get to their houses.

One day I decided to walk around the camp and on coming to the Wall I walked up the access road. Except for a couple of young kids, there was no-one else around. Suddenly I heard a metal clanging. It took me a few moments to realize that it was coming from a watchtower in the Wall. I didn't have my camera out and clearly presented no threat so I decided to walk at an unhurried pace up the road. Then I heard a loud crack and turned to see some form of munition, thrown from the watchtower, sparking and smoking on the ground. I ducked into an alleyway guided by a boy and we sat down, sheltered by a housing block. It was break time in the UN school next to the alleyway. Kids were playing outside in the shadow of the watchtower. I crept over to the school wall and took the photo opposite. The boy said "Be careful. The soldiers are watching." After 20 minutes we left the alleyway, quickly making our way down the access road and into another side street away from the Wall. I thought, "I'm glad I'm not Palestinian. I'm so lucky I can go home."

The author

Checkpoint watchtower in the
Wall overlooking a school in
Ayda refugee camp, Bethlehem

Passageway in the Old City, Nablus. The narrow streets of the Old City have enabled Palestinians in Nablus to resist the Israelis more effectively than in other towns and consequently the Israelis impose their stranglehold through means of checkpoints surrounding the city.

The great land grab

The situation in Palestine is usually portrayed as complex and ever changing, as a story too random and fluid to be interpreted. It is in Israel's interest to portray it in this way because where policies cannot be deduced, they cannot be criticized. In reality, Israel has consistently pursued a policy of land confiscation from Palestinians since its creation, a policy which is as active now as it has ever been.

During the early years of Zionism a fiction was constructed that Palestine was an empty land ready for the establishment of a Jewish state. This was summed up by an early Zionist, Israel Zangwill, who termed it "A land without people for a people without land". By the early twentieth century it was, however, widely understood within the movement that there was a significant Arab population in Palestine and that some solution needed to be found to free land for Jewish settlement. The solution was Ben Gurion's ethnic cleansing policy. Prior to the 1948 War 93% of land in Palestine belonged to Arabs. However, the land owned or leased by the refugees who fled their homes during the *nakba* was confiscated and transferred to quasi-governmental organizations like the Jewish National Fund. The JNF holds land for the benefit of Jews worldwide, not the citizens of Israel, thereby excluding Israeli Palestinians. Palestinian land ownership was reduced to only 7% by the confiscations.

While the Palestinians, as individuals and families, physically retain land they have hope. Without the link to land, they begin to lose their identity. The destruction of the collective Palestinian identity has been central to Israeli policy since 1948. The Palestinians were originally a pastoral people living off the land but for most refugees, forced off their land and into camps in 1948, that link has been broken. This process has continued since 1967, as West Bank Palestinians have increasingly been restricted to urban areas. An urban population is more subject to economic hardship and more mobile. As the land disappears the pressure builds on Palestinians to emigrate. In the absence of Palestinians, new settlements redefine the landscape, names are judaized and history is rewritten – now there is a land without people for a people without land.

Article 49 of the fourth Geneva Convention states that "The Occupying Power shall not deport or transfer parts of its own civilian population into the territory it occupies." The establishment and expansion of Israeli settlements in the West Bank and Gaza Strip have been declared violations of the fourth Geneva Convention by the UN Security Council in resolutions 446, 452, 465 and 471, an opinion confirmed by the International Court of Justice.

The first settlements established after Israel's occupation of the West Bank were

Settlement in the hills above
Bethlehem, viewed from
Deheisheh Refugee Camp

removed by the Israeli government while it was still debating the territory's future. However, it did not take long for them to be officially sanctioned and incorporated within the Israeli mechanism for control of the West Bank. Of course, Israel could quite easily exercise its control of the West Bank through military means alone. However, the Zionist movement had always sought to incorporate the West Bank into Israel and it found a willing partner in Menachem Begin, elected to Prime Minister in 1977. He authorized settlement building throughout the territory, couching his arguments in nationalistic and religious terms rather than strategic and security ones.

Despite consistent criticism of settlement building and expansion by the international community including even the US, and commitments by Israel not to suspend building, Israel has forged ahead with an aggressive colonization of East Jerusalem and the West Bank since 1977. Israel has worked to a predefined plan to establish large settlement blocks on Palestinian territory adjacent to its internationally accepted border. It is a common misconception that Yasser Arafat rejected a fair settlement offered by Prime Minister Barak (and Bill Clinton) at Camp David in 2000. In reality, Barak built settlements faster than any other Israeli Prime Minister, increasing numbers by 90% and only offered to withdraw 20% of them, which would have left 180,000 settlers in 209 settlements on 10% of West Bank land. During the last decade Israel has restricted itself to large-scale expansion of existing settlements, but in December 2006 it announced a new settlement, Meskiot, would be built in the Jordan valley. There are currently approximately 450,000 settlers in the West Bank, 180,000 of whom are in East Jerusalem and 270,000 in the rest of the West Bank, up 6 six per cent in 2006 alone.

The building of settlements and associated land confiscation, together with the status of Jerusalem and refugees, are the most divisive issues between Israel and the Palestinians. Israel has used settlements to strengthen its hold on the West Bank. Its settlement policy has been used as a tool to effect an annexation of West Bank territory. With every confiscation and subsequent building of settlement infrastructure, the Palestinians see their opportunity for their own state slipping away.

Confiscation increasingly takes the form of a military confiscation order which is followed by re-zoning for settlement, then confiscation of surrounding farmland for settler farms and roads, and future expansion. For many years the Israeli courts sanctioned confiscations on the basis of the right under international law for an occupier to use land temporarily for security purposes, even though the nature of settlement is permanent. The next land confiscation was then justified on the basis of the security needs of the new settlement, thereby setting up an unending, circular process. Ultimately, the Supreme Court found it could not continue this fiction, although it did not require any land

Street in the Old City, Hebron showing debris thrown from settlers who have illegally occupied the upper floors of the houses. The netting offers some protection to Palestinians below.

confiscated previously to be returned. However, Israel then fell back on absentee landownership provisions to confiscate lands. As an occupying force, it is obliged to use existing Jordanian law but does so only when it is to its benefit. Jordanian law incorporated the Ottoman concept of *miri*. This stated that land which was unused for three years would revert to state land. Israel consequently took existing state land for itself and has since used every opportunity to enforce the provisions, often manufacturing abandonment by restricting Palestinian access to land or making cultivation uneconomic. It is very likely that these provisions will be applied to the large amount of Palestinian land deliberately separated from its owners by the Wall. During the Mandate period a system of land registration was developed but it was implemented slowly and by 1967, when Israel stopped the process, only 34% of land in the West Bank had been registered. Consequently much land ownership was evidenced only by Ottoman documents or by village knowledge. Israel has taken advantage of this lack of evidence by confiscating land and obliging the owners to prove their title in Israeli courts. This is an expensive process beyond the means of many Palestinians.

The Jewish National Fund has extended its reach into the West Bank. To disguise its activities, it acquires Palestinian land through a private company called Himnuta, of which it owns 99%. Despite this fact, and its Jew-only land use policy, the JNF still continues to raise money for further land purchases through a registered charity in the UK and a not-for-profit corporation in the USA, both of which remain entitled to tax relief. Tony Blair and David Cameron, the leader of the main British opposition party, are both honorary patrons of the JNF Charitable Trust.

Israel's land confiscation, settlement and planning policies impact on the Palestinians in three main ways. Firstly, they are an open manifestation of Israel's intention to retain (at least) significant portions of the West Bank and deny the Palestinians a viable state. Secondly, they deprive individuals of sources of livelihood and room for natural expansion. Thirdly, on a daily basis their presence and activities confirm to Palestinians their sub-status as subjugated people.

Where Palestinian land cannot be easily confiscated or is not yet required by the Israeli state, Israel uses its powers under the Oslo Accords to restrict its development. Much open land falls into Area C under the Accords and is therefore under Israeli administrative control. Israeli authorities refuse permission for Palestinians to build in Area C or develop commercial or agricultural infrastructure, thereby making their products less competitive, and denying them natural room for expansion and the opportunity to create their own facts on the ground. In the past ten years, the Israeli authorities have demolished more than 2,200 homes, leaving more than 13,000 Palestinians homeless. The houses are normally demolished at night without warning.

A fenced section of the "Wall" taking a long deviation to include the land covered by olive trees on the Israeli side while excluding the houses of their Palestinians owners (including Ibrahim (see page 140)).

Settlers themselves are drawn to the West Bank for differing reasons. In established settlements, particularly close to Jerusalem, cheaper house prices and rents and, at one time, tax incentives encouraged ordinary Israelis to move to settlements. The vanguard of the settlement movement, however, is made up of radical Jews, often from America, who claim a historical and biblical right to the territory. One leading rabbi within the settler movement told his followers:

"I tell you explicitly that the Torah forbids us to surrender even one inch of our liberated land. There are no conquests here and we are not occupying foreign lands; we are returning to our home, to the inheritance of our ancestors. There is no Arab land here, only the inheritance of our God – and the more the world gets used to this thought the better it will be for them and for all of us."

It is these radicals who predominate in the smaller, newer settlements close to areas of Palestinian population. Israel depends on them to build new bridgeheads in the West Bank which it can then link with other settlements. With full state support, including protection from the IDF, they work to clear areas of land by intimidating local Palestinians. The Israeli government aids the process by creating obstacles which threaten traditional Palestinian patterns of life, for example by building barriers beside roads to prevent Palestinians herding animals. Settlers are subject to Israeli law and can commit acts of violence against Palestinians with relative impunity. There are countless examples of settlers killing and wounding Palestinians working their fields adjacent to settlements, and of settlers intimidating Palestinians until they vacate their lands and homes. Sometimes the Israeli police intervene but if so, it is only to stop a particular incident at a particular time. With no real sanction applied against them and the protection of the Israeli army, settlers are free to continue intimidation over a number of years until the Palestinian will breaks.

Settlers have considerable influence within Israeli politics. The withdrawal from Gaza shows that in reality settlements could probably be dismantled by the Israeli government if it decided to do so (provided it could carry its electorate with it). We are, of course, talking of many thousands of people but many of these are economic, not ideological, settlers who would respond to financial incentives. The routing of the Wall deep into Palestinian territory to enclose major settlement blocks has resulted in only 70,000 of 450,000 settlers remaining on the West Bank side and the Israeli government may be looking forward to a time when the outlying settlements are abandoned. However, Israel has given no indication that it intends to follow such a path.

Houses overlooking a park in Ma'ale Adumim. Ma'ale Adumim is one of the biggest settlements in the West Bank, housing in excess of 25,000 people – most of whom work in Jerusalem. It is still expanding.

"Settlers regularly come to the gates of the school and fire shots into it. Once, a settler called Amnon entered the school and shot and injured a pupil. I pursued him through the Israeli courts and on conviction his gun was taken away from him for one month…

…but I have another story I'd rather you tell. Once I noticed a disturbance outside the school. When I arrived a group of soldiers were arguing with some teachers. One soldier came up to me and said, "I hate you because you are an Arab."

I replied: "I hate you, but not because you are a Jew, because you are a Zionist."

A Palestinian state within the 1967 borders would be acceptable to most Palestinians. Settlers are the problem – they are on our land."

Tawfiq, former headmaster, Ya'bad

Tawfiq, former headmaster, Ya'bad

Ibrahim, a refugee living near Bethlehem, took me over to the fence which Israel has erected on his land, separating him from his olive groves. The fence is part of the barrier (the Wall) which Israel has erected to separate the settlement blocks that it intends to annex from the rest of the West Bank. We were standing by it for a minute, maybe two, talking. Suddenly an Israeli jeep swept down the road on the other side of the fence and then instructed us by megaphone to move away. I quickly took the photo opposite. Ibrahim later explained:

"My family were originally from Beit Natif, now in Israel. In 1948 news came that Israelis were destroying villages, raping women, killing children so it was better for people to leave and return when the Arab army arrived. They expected to be away for one week, maybe a month. After 60 years we are still refugees.

My grandfather came to Ayda camp and in 1991 the family bought land in Beit Sahour from a man whose family had owned it for centuries – he was 70. We had the Ottoman papers to prove it.

The Israelis served us with notice that they wanted to build a road. First it was six metres. After that, more papers, more land. We were told to go to Court if we disagreed. In 2002 the road was made much bigger. They put up a fence so we couldn't access our lands. They did it at the same time as the Bethlehem siege so people wouldn't notice.

The municipality asked for permission for us to access our olives but were refused. I was never offered any money. I know some others were but they wouldn't accept it because it was a small amount and would mean they would be seen as collaborators. We lost 17 dunums [4.2 acres] in all."

Minutes later the jeep, joined by another, stopped on the road (which snakes around Ibrahim's house adjacent to the fence, and called for us to come out of the house. Ibrahim explained I was a journalist. The border guard said, "You are the person who is living here so you have to watch yourself. As you know your house is between being destroyed and not destroyed. If you keep far away from the fence and keep your children away and keep calm and quiet everything will be ok." We went back inside and Ibrahim said:

"The border guards watch us 24 hours a day because that's their job. We are already refugees. Now we are being moved on again. My kids know not to go near the fence. When they do, the guards come in their jeeps and shout at them. I say to them, "why do you frighten four- and five-year-old children? When they are older they can throw stones but now they can do nothing. Even if they could get through the first fence there is another and another." You know I think it makes them happy. I think they are scared and it makes them feel powerful."

The author

Ibrahim looks through the Israeli security fence separating him from his olive trees in the valley below.

"We have 100 acres but are fighting for 300 because our neighbours' lands stem from the same title. Six years ago we decided to invite people to our farm from all over the world. We wanted to prevent our land being confiscated. There has been a court case in process for fifteen years since 1991. My uncle and his father before him owned this land. Our lawyer has had to go to Turkey and London to search records and now we have the papers to prove our title but that is no guarantee against confiscation. It has cost us over US$100,000 to date. As the settlers have no evidence the Court keeps adjourning the case rather than rule against them.

In 2002, settlers attacked us with a big bulldozer intending to build a road through our land. They cut down 250 olive trees and broke all our water tanks. I said to them, "This is my land." The settlers responded "God promised us this land. This is our land." I managed to stop the bulldozer for one hour and the police put me in prison for one day for my trouble.

Palestinians want freedom and peace and to live for the future. We don't want to drive the Israelis into the sea. We have some idiots of course who get involved in shooting but they are a small minority.

Land for us is the future. If we have no land, we have no future."

Daher, Nahallin

Wall painting of a Palestinian
family's ancestors, copied from
an old photograph by Paul Gent,
an English voluntary worker

"We have about 5,000 people in Jifflick. There are two schools but the high school is housed in tents. The building of the school was to be funded by the US after Saeb Erakat [a Palestinian negotiator] brought a representative from the US consulate to see the school but it has been stopped because of the US boycott. We have 20,000 dunums [4,940 acres], 32 wells and a spring. In the winter we supply 75% of the total agricultural products produced in the West Bank. It is valuable land so the Israelis made it Area C so they can keep control. They don't want Jifflick to become a small city. It is all registered land but we are not allowed to build.

We consider ourselves closer to Nablus than Jericho – Nablus is our market. We can travel to Nablus but nobody from Nablus can get here without a permit. Now we have to tow our tractors to Jericho for repair. We have had no access to the hills since 1967 because they are closed military zones so we can't graze our animals. We can't build any new infrastructure – water pipes or electricity supplies. We have to use generators. If we want to sell milk or cheese, often it goes bad at checkpoints because we can't preserve it. We can't build pens or sheds for the protection of animals or produce as the Israelis come and destroy them. I built a shed for 120 sheep. It cost me 100,000 shekels [US$22,220] but the Israelis destroyed it and therefore I had to sell my sheep.

There are people living in Guantanamo so people can live here. Everything is forbidden here – next you will need a permit to sleep with your wife! The international community are interested in helping but every time someone wants to donate, the Israeli authorities stop them. An occupying power has a responsibility to provide. Not only are they not providing, they are stopping others."

Council President, Jifflick, Jordan Valley

Council President standing by his livestock shed, demolished by the Israeli authorities, Jifflick in the Jordan Valley

Two Palestinian boys crossing an Israeli-only settlement road to reach their village, Qawawis. The Israeli authorities have now built a concrete wall adjacent to the road to prevent livestock crossing. One of the Israeli settlements surrounding the village can be seen in the background.

"We went to a wedding in Karmel for a week in 2001 and during that time a settler came, burnt all our possessions and occupied our cave. In 2002 the Courts made him leave after we engaged an Israeli lawyer for 7,000 shekels [US$1,550]. The settler filled the cave with stones when he left which cost 1,000 shekels [US$220] of labour to remove.

We bought the land in 1960 as we had rented a previous house. We carved out the cave ourselves and it was meant to be a storeroom but when the Israelis came in 1967 they didn't allow us to build homes so we lived in the cave. We managed to extend it to make room for our children.

The settlers come down to the village and dance and clap hands shouting "we are going to live here" or "aren't you going to offer us bread and tea?" They used to come every Friday and Saturday – now they come any time. Some dress up in army uniform and try to come in our door. They have guns. The only thing that stops them is the presence of volunteers from the International Solidarity Movement – they are afraid of photos because they know the law is on our side. They came last week. The police come sometimes and tell them to leave."

Ibrahim and Fatima, Qawawis

Author's note

On a visit to Qawawis in January 2007, Ibrahim explained to me that the settlers had now restricted the villagers to grazing within 100 metres of their village. The implication was clear. They were on borrowed time.

Since writing the paragraph above, on 14 February 2007, the IDF has demolished all the houses in Qawawis (numbering four or five), belonging to Ibrahim and Fatima's neighbours, and houses in three other nearby villages. This is a demonstration of how quickly Israel's policy of dispossession and ethnic cleansing is being implemented.

For further information or to make a donation towards the rebuilding of the houses, see the International Solidarity Movement website (www.palsolidarity.org).

Ibrahim and Fatima, Qawawis

Hebron is a city of great religious significance as both Muslims and Jews believe Abraham is buried here. It is also one of the West Bank's largest cities, home to 160,000 Palestinians. Jews had a small presence in Hebron's Old City between the expulsion of the Jews from Spain in 1492 and 1936 when the British removed them because of increasing sectarian violence. In one incident 67 Jews and 24 Arabs were killed. Most of their properties were sold to Arabs but those which remained were taken over by the Absentee Property Department. In 1979 permission was given to settlers to return to these properties. The arrival of these settlers, who are some of the most fanatical and aggressive in the West Bank, increased tension with killings on both sides. On 25 February 1994 settlers killed 29 Palestinians and injured a further 11 in the Abraham mosque.

In 1997 the city's security responsibilities were divided, with the IDF retaining control of the Old City so they could protect 400 settlers in an area of 40,000 Palestinians. During the second *intifada*, Palestinians were placed under curfew for 600 days in three years. Twenty-two entrances to the Old City were blocked. 800 Palestinian shops were forced to close and a further 2,000 closed because of the access restrictions. Many people left, leaving 100 families at best. Since 1996, the Hebron Rehabilitation Committee has been working to restore buildings and repopulate the area. However, its work is restricted because of settlement expansion plans.

Around 400 to 500 settlers live in the settlement in the Old City, which is split into five areas. The areas in between are still Palestinian. However, Israel is trying to drive out the Palestinians remaining there. They are not permitted to open shops in the area. In any case, they would have little custom as non-resident Palestinians are not permitted in these areas. Some Palestinian residents are not permitted to leave their houses on the Jewish sabbath.

In the 1990s settlers broke into a shop in the old vegetable market and made it into an apartment. In 2004, the Court issued a decision asking the army and police to evict the settlers. However, the Ministry of Defence issued a letter asking them to postpone enforcement. In 2005 the settlers voluntarily evacuated half of the building and kept the other half.

Between 1999 and 2005, settlers broke into a family house three times through a shared wall. A court order was obtained and the police removed them in each case. Then in 2006 they broke in again and the police refused to act without a further court order.

In one instance settlers threw petrol bombs at a house, destroyed its kitchen and incorporated the land into the settlement. The owners went to court, which issued judgment in their favour, but after four years they are still waiting for the Israeli police to enforce it.

The author

A Palestinian area between areas of Israeli settlement in the Old City of Hebron, where residents are not permitted to open their shops or receive Palestinian visitors, and a passageway in the Old City blocked by the Israeli authorities

The Wall at Abu Dis, on the West
Bank side, blocking a main road
into Jerusalem

Business and agriculture

Since 1967, Israel has followed a policy of destabilising the economy of the West Bank in order to preclude Palestinian economic autonomy and prevent competition with the Israeli economy. Its success can be measured by the fact that the agricultural sector, traditionally the bedrock of the Palestinian economy and its major source of employment, formed only 6.4% of Gross Domestic Product in 2003. With the economies of scale and modern production techniques available to large companies in Israel, Palestinian producers would struggle to compete in normal circumstances. However, the additional pressures applied by their occupiers make it impossible. Many Palestinian enterprises have gone out of business. For example, once there were 43 soap makers in Nablus, a city famed the world over for the quality of its soaps made from pure olive oil; now there are three. Many Palestinians with financial resources sufficient to set up businesses have emigrated.

The 2.5 million Palestinians in the West Bank are an important market for Israeli companies, for which the West Bank is a duty-free zone, and Israel has no interest in allowing the development of competition from West Bank producers. It restricts the import of raw materials and the issue of licences for establishment of businesses. Israel has tried to restrict international aid to Palestinian farmers on the basis that West Bank production will damage the Israeli farm economy. West Bank companies have to abide by Israeli law, which is applied to the letter to place the maximum burden upon them. For example, a Palestinian farmer in the Jordan Valley explained to me that the Israeli nature conservation authority would only allow him to remove trees if they were replanted elsewhere on his land. However, the settlers farming the neighbouring, confiscated land had removed all non-farming related vegetation with no sanction. Pressure is applied to force companies to purchase Israeli supplies. Goods can sit in customs for weeks awaiting clearance. When exporting to Jordan, the Israeli authorities require everything to be unloaded and loaded on to another truck.

The disruption caused by restrictions on movement makes it very difficult for producers to operate. For example, farmers wishing to transport produce to Nablus require two permits – one to leave the Jordan Valley and one to enter Nablus. The many checkpoints impact severely on business. Products can be held up at the whim of a soldier. Often the entire load has to be taken off for inspection. It is impossible to guarantee shipments of perishable goods. In the summer, with temperatures often above 37°C (100°F), products perish very quickly. This limits many farmers to their local markets and depresses prices. The prohibition on travel to the Jordan Valley by Palestinians from other areas of the West Bank means the valley's farmers must tow their

Opposite

Restaurant and leisure venture on the outskirts of Nablus, forced out of business at the beginning of the first *intifada* because of a nearby road closure by the IDF and the killing of Palestinians in the area by Israeli snipers located in Israeli settlements

tractors out of the valley, up to 15 miles up mountain roads, to have them repaired.

Restrictions on building near farmland in Area C prevent Palestinians from establishing processing facilities. Consequently Palestine, the land of fruits, imports jam. Businesses find it difficult to obtain supplies which Israelis deem as a potential security threat, for example sodium hydroxide, an essential ingredient in soap. The sanctions imposed by the West after the election of Hamas to government have allowed Israel to impose such restrictions more widely, for example, preventing the supply of used oil to one company whose business is based on refining it. Outdated facilities, restrictions on movement of employees and products, and uncertainties in the supply chain are part of everyday life. However, in the modern world such inefficiencies are brutally exploited by the market and new businesses cannot be expected to survive when faced with the extra costs and uncertainties of operating under occupation.

Bethlehem is in a desperate situation. A large proportion of its population used to derive their incomes from tourism, many from carving souvenirs or working in the hotel trade. However, very few tourists visit Bethlehem now and when they do, they are often bussed in from Israeli hotels in Jerusalem. One hotel owner said to me:

"One litre of kerosene costs US$1 – the same as in Israel but we have no income. We can't afford to heat the hotel. The Israeli average income is US$17,000 – we have nothing. Water and electricity is very expensive – it comes from Israel – we are paying them for our own water. We are given ten permits to visit Jerusalem for our business but what's the point if we have no money to spend. The most important issue is that there is no access to jobs. The EU tried to get people to take loans but it's like trying to resurrect a dead person – they wanted security! People have no hope."

Hundreds of thousands of Palestinian olive trees have been destroyed and a vast quantity of agricultural land confiscated due to the development of Israeli infrastructure – the Wall, roads, military installations and settlements. Where land remains, farmers may be denied access or face intimidation from nearby settlements. Many Palestinian farmers have been killed while tending their crops and livestock farmers are increasingly prevented from moving herds across traditional pastureland.

Limits on the supply of and the price of water, which Israel controls, restrict the ability of farmers to farm. One of the main reasons why Israel wishes to keep control of the West Bank is so it can keep control of the West Bank's water supplies. The northern West Bank sits on large aquifers which Israel depends on to meet its population's Western water usage patterns. It has strategically built one of its largest settlements, Ariel, on one of these aquifers. It has also annexed a part of the northern West Bank where many wells are located by routing the Wall around them. Israel takes 80% of West Bank, Palestinian water for itself while preventing Palestinian farmers from drilling new wells. Instead it sells

Money changer in Ramallah
counting Israeli shekels, the
currency imposed by Israel when
it occupied the West Bank

them their own water for four times the price at which it is supplied to Israeli settlements. In the Jordan Valley where some Palestinian farmers depend on rainwater to replenish their wells, they are not permitted to enter the nearby hills to clean the valleys which feed them while settlers "green the desert" (Palestinian land) using Palestinian water. Taking into account industrial water use, Israeli water consumption is five and a half times that of Palestinians. Palestinian towns and villages frequently face water cuts and have to buy water off trailers while settlers have unrestricted access to water allowing them to enjoy parks, sports fields and swimming pools.

Gordon Brown, the British finance minister and possible next Prime Minister, has recently talked of moving the Palestinian-Israeli situation forward by promoting enterprise and economic development in the West Bank, a pipedream given Israel's consistent and deliberate obstruction in this area. Given that his advisers are well acquainted with the facts on the ground, his statement is an example of how western politicians take advantage of the Israeli-Palestinian conflict to boost their stature at home, irrespective of the actual realities.

Palestinian agricultural workers in
the Jordan valley

"We opened Taybeh Brewery in August 1995. Taybeh in Arabic means delicious. We've developed our own recipe according to the 1516 German purity law. Belgian and French malt is crushed on site and we use Bavarian and Czech hops. We came back to Palestine to invest, to set an example, not to wait for EU money.

Business is not as good since 2000. Jordan has imposed a 181% tax to protect Jordanian Amstel. Israel is not buying so much because there is less tourism. Palestinian people have lost pride in their own products because of the occupation. Also, we cannot sell in Muslim areas such as Gaza, Jenin and Nablus as the Palestinian Authority won't issue licences. We have high hopes, that's all we have.

We have to get export permits through the PA who clear it with the Israelis, or directly from the Israelis. For five weeks now we have prepared a new batch for shipment for Japan and failed to clear customs. We are waiting for a shipment of hops from Germany. We have paid the import tax. However, last week our application was sent back as it was in English, not Hebrew. Then they said they needed a photocopy of the sanitary certificate. I still don't know when it will arrive. We are out of hops. On its arrival health checks will mean another four to five weeks wait.

I used to buy boxes from a Palestinian company in Nablus. The Israelis wouldn't allow them to cross the checkpoint though so now I have to buy from Israel. I used to buy bottles from Portugal. They were fine but now they don't meet Israeli "tests" so again I must buy from Israel.

It is not asking for much – we just want to live like human beings. We want to be able to take our kids to school easily and not for it to take all day. We want to send our father and mother for medical treatment, not for them to die at checkpoints. It is all a deliberate attempt to make people leave the country.

Last week my niece was turned back from Tel Aviv airport while travelling on an American passport. They handcuffed her and said she lied about having a Palestinian passport. She didn't have that passport on her, it wasn't renewed. Where are the human rights? They said Palestinians must come through the back door – across Allenby Bridge from Jordan. They treat us like animals."

Nadim Khoury, proprietor of Taybeh Brewery

Nadim Khoury, proprietor of
Taybeh Brewery

"Last week there was an incident at five or six in the evening. An 18 year-old carrying eggs through the checkpoint was shot. He had 30 bullets in him. The Israelis say they were shot at. There were no witnesses.

Five metal doors now enclose the old city. If anything happens the Israelis can now lock us in the city. There has been no curfew for the twenty days since the doors were installed but between 2000 and 2004 we had curfews lasting a fortnight and even a month. We used to sneak out back passages for food but now they are blocked.

I have had to move my shop because settlers occupying the upper floors of my building were throwing rubbish down on us. I am renting from a shopkeeper who has moved out. Now there are only 50 to 60 shops in the old city. There used to be about 3,000. The population of the Old City before 1967 was over 60,000. Now it is about 5,000.

Sometimes I sit outside my shop from eight in the morning to three in the afternoon without any customers. I need 100 shekels [US$22] a day for my family. Many have left to find better jobs. There is increasing theft amongst Palestinians because there is no work. The Israelis and Palestinian Authority do nothing. The Palestinian Authority can't come into the Old City because it is under Israeli control."

Jamal, shopkeeper, Hebron

Jamal, shopkeeper, Hebron

A Palestinian greenhouse which Khalid, a farmer from Anabta, cannot use because of lack of water. Israel regulates supply and prohibits Palestinians from digging new wells. Settlements are often built on top of aquifers to control supply. Water consumption by the 5,000 settlers and their farming activities in the Jordan valley alone is equal to 75% of the amount consumed by the two and a half million Palestinians in the West Bank. 80% of water from the West Bank goes to Israel and its settlements.

10 | Unemployment, poverty and health

"People are poor and need support but I disagree with aid. The Palestinian problem is not a humanitarian one. We have the most qualified, highly educated people in the Middle East – we need to create small projects that can create jobs. Giving people the impression that help will come from outside and that Palestinians need do nothing is a bad thing – it keeps us in the devil's circle."

Daoud

For 30 years after 1967 the West Bank acted as a labour pool for Israel. To a great extent, Palestinians built the modern infrastructure of Israel and its settlements, and at one point, a third of the Palestinian workforce worked in Israel, accounting for 42% of Palestinian GDP through remittances. As detailed in the previous chapter, at the same time, Israel suffocated the Palestinian economy. During the second *intifada* Israel discarded this labour force in favour of foreign migrant workers mostly from the Far East. Israel's reoccupation of the West Bank in 2002 destroyed much Palestinian infrastructure and further weakened the economy. The suspension of aid by the US and Europe and the withholding of customs revenues by Israel has deprived the PA of US$1.9 billion annually, and has meant that it has been unable to pay fully the salaries of 140,000 employees including doctors and policeman. In the absence of these incomes, the Authority's services and institutions are falling apart as employees refuse to work without pay.

Many Palestinians are finding it difficult to maintain normal patterns of life. Medical bills become problems, university fees become prohibitive. Many find it a struggle to pay the high prices of Israeli-supplied electricity and gas. In December 2006 unemployment in the West Bank stood at 23.4% of the labour force. Many of those who are employed are extremely poorly paid and those who are unemployed, mostly young men, face a state of perpetual unemployment. 43.2% of the population was living in deep poverty (with incomes of less than US$1 per day) in mid-2006. However, many families have some sort of safety net. Large families are expensive to support but also increase the chances of there being one member with a job good enough to provide some support for others. In 2004 every working Palestinian supported 6.4 non-working people. A large number of Palestinians work abroad in other Arab countries while family members in the diaspora also contribute. The UN supports the refugee population with basic food rations, medical care and schooling. Some, however, fall through the net, like the boy pictured on a burning rubbish dump in Tulkarm at the end of this chapter. In one survey 30% of children under five years old who were screened suffered from chronic malnutrition and 21% from acute malnutrition.

There are also a great many NGOs operating in the West Bank. At the basic level of supporting the population with its basic needs, they often do a valuable job and before the establishment of the Palestinian Authority they were the only mechanism for such support. Their contribution has, however, disguised the total neglect by Israel of its

international obligations under the Geneva Convention to meet the humanitarian needs of the Palestinians. This was despite the massive contribution that the Palestinian workforce made to the Israeli economy and the continuing contribution it is making as a market for Israeli goods. A significant proportion of these NGOs are Islamic charities and they have been particularly important in helping the vulnerable during the international boycott. However, Israel has used claims of links with militants to limit their activities. Between May and August 2006, 37 of them were targeted in IDF attacks, searches and raids.

Under the Oslo Accords, the Palestinian Authority accepted responsibility for supporting Palestinians under its control but Israeli restrictions, international sanctions and internal inefficiencies and corruption make its task very difficult. NGOs are now competing with the PA, providing services which the PA should be looking to provide. Many government-funded NGOs place restrictions on the provision of aid, which mean they cannot integrate well with the PA's service provision. For example, they may insist on the provision of services by their own foreign nationals rather than Palestinians or the purchase of their own national products. The development of the PA's own functions are therefore inevitably being hampered to some degree.

Access to medical services in the West Bank is unpredictable. Palestinian ambulances are not permitted to use settler roads and therefore must take longer, indirect routes to their destinations. They are frequently held at checkpoints with patients awaiting urgent medical care. Many hospitals are short of important drugs, and treatment for complex or unusual conditions must often be sought in Jordan. 2,500 Palestinians were permanently disabled during the second *intifada* but rehabilitation and care for them is very poor. The medical situation is exacerbated by environmental pollution caused by Israeli factories and settlements, and Israeli restrictions on the development of Palestinian waste disposal infrastructure. The United Nations Occupied Palestinian Territories Mid Year Review, 2005 states:

"In the absence of IDF permits to construct solid waste landfill sites, and other alternatives, local authorities continue to dump solid waste and untreated waste water on the outskirts of towns and villages and in wadis [watercourses] contributing to the pollution of groundwater. There have also been problems in a number of areas with waste water from Israeli settlements polluting Palestinian water sources."

However, as the quote at the start of this chapter alludes to, it should be remembered that the Palestinian problem is not a humanitarian one but a political one. It is about the denial of the rights of freedom, justice and self-determination. The humanitarian aspects follow on as consequence. Having said that, they do contribute significantly to the Quiet Transfer.

Two girls walking down a typical
street in a West Bank refugee
camp, Qalandia refugee camp

"I worked in Israel in Ramat Gan near Tel Aviv in a meat and chicken factory for twenty years. Now the Israelis have replaced us with Russians and Chinese. Every man in this camp used to work in Israel. Now they get sick because they worry too much – how to get money, how to support their children.

I am 55 and have ten children. Two have grown up and left the house. Four boys share one bedroom, four girls in the other. My wife and I sleep in the living room. One boy is disabled.

Before, you could help yourself, but now we are down to zero. If children ask for fruit we can't give it to them. We can't afford medicine for our child. He needs 24 capsules a day. We have one boy in university – it is very expensive."

Abdul, unemployed refugee, New Askar refugee camp, Nablus

Author's note

Jamil, one of Abdul's sons (pictured crouching down), has since been killed by the IDF (see page 122). Abdul found out about his son's death within one hour of discovering that another son, suffering from a leg condition that forced him to use a wheelchair, had had a successful operation in Jordan.

Abdul, an unemployed refugee, with his family, New Askar refugee camp, Nablus

"In 2000 I went to work in the [adjacent] Israeli settlement illegally. One day I was painting a window in a settler house when I was shot in the arm by the police – until now I still don't know why. The violence against us is getting worse. I get up at 3 a.m. to get into the settlement – sometimes I stay all week."

Builder, southern West Bank

Builder, southern West Bank

"This was the best area in Tulkarm before the chemical factories were built – best for agriculture, trade and air. This was the Road of Kings. You could be in Qalqilya in 15 minutes. Now the road is blocked by the Wall and the journey takes one hour.

The factories were moved from Israel in 1985 because of local opposition. They are built on the Palestinian side of the Green Line. They took the land illegally. No one knew what products were produced initially. Now there are seven factories – the insecticide and gas ones are the most dangerous. It operates night and day except for the Jewish Sabbath and when the wind is blowing towards Israel. There are tax concessions for Israelis who set up business here. They are Israeli-owned but use Palestinian labour working under Jordanian law with little protection. Now workers have no choice but to work there.

My children are suffering from eye infections. Fortunately they haven't got cancer. We can't open windows. My family are from Jaffa. The Israelis forced us out in 1948 and we moved to Jbarah which is now isolated behind the Wall. I moved here and the chemical plant was built. The Israelis keep following us – we can't keep moving.

The Israelis have issued an order to demolish a neighbour's building because it's in front of the chemical factory and could be used as a base to attack it. Nobody is renting his property. His child is suffering from asthma and goes to hospital three days every month."

Adib, mechanic

"I don't have exact statistics but in the last ten to fifteen years the incidence of cancer in the parts of the Palestinian Territories neighbouring Israel, especially Jenin, Tulkarm and Qalqilya, has increased. There are a lot of settlements near Qalqilya and between Salfit and Qalqilya. All polluting industries have been transferred from Israel to the West Bank. It may be that Palestinian farmers are not using insecticides correctly due to lack of education. Tulkarm, Jenin and Qalqilya are agricultural areas producing a lot of fruit and vegetables. It could be that people are taking viral medication in incorrect dosages. What I am sure of is there is a very aggressive polluting agent in the Tulkarm sky. I have operated on nine children with advanced Non-Hodgkin lymphoma in one year."

Doctor, Tulkarm hospital

Adib and members of his family outside their house, which lies next to Israeli chemical factories. The photograph was taken on the Jewish sabbath when the factory was not operating.

"Nahallin is now surrounded by four settlements. Before 1967 Nahallin had 30,000 dunums [7,410 acres] of land, in 1967 this was reduced to 14,000, now it is 7,000, and the latest confiscation order will leave 3,000 [741 acres] remaining. The Israelis are confiscating the land to build a road between settlements, but they have been trying to force us off it for years. When there is a problem with the settlement's sewage system they channel the waste on to our fields. It has contaminated one of our two springs and much of our remaining land.

The town with a population of 7,000 and rising cannot expand beyond its 1,100 dunums as the adjacent land is Area C and therefore under Israeli control according to the Oslo Agreement. We used to have three roads we could use to access the town. Now we are only allowed one and this will soon only be accessible through a gate.

There has been an increase in breast and blood cancer. More die from cancer than old age. My sister is suffering. We try to find reason but we need a scientist. Perhaps it is vegetables grown on the contaminated land. Perhaps high-voltage cables. There is usually a long delay before diagnosis so it is very difficult to stop. We only have a little clinic here."

Mohammed, Nahallin, a town located in the

Etzian enclave between the Wall and the Green Line

Mural on a municipal building
destroyed in an IDF attack,
Ramallah

Palestinian boy scavenging on a
rubbish dump, Tulkarm

11 | Childhood and education

The young people of Palestine are born into despair. Their parents have known better times and, despite the desperateness of the situation, this knowledge offers a fragment of hope for some to cling to. Their children, however, are born into an environment where killings, imprisonment and destruction are everyday events. Many grow up in impoverished households with limited access to healthcare, and poor nutrition. The situation is particularly bad for refugee children who live in overcrowded camps, who see and hear the IDF operating in their camps night after night, and who treat as normal the killing of relatives, friends and classmates. Over 800 children have been killed since 2000. 4,000 children were arrested and detained between September 2000 and April 2006. Today, 321 children remain in Israeli jails, some as young as twelve.

But what effect does this have on them in the long term? I was walking around Qalandia refugee camp on the morning of Eid Al-Adha, the main Muslim festival, in January 2007. Men were crowded around butchers, waiting for their sheep to be slaughtered, according to the Islamic ritual, before distributing the meat to the needy. Meanwhile, their young sons were racing around the camp playing with their new toys – without exception, plastic guns. In towns all over the West Bank, computer cafes have sprung up, crammed with kids playing on violent computer games.

If this was the UK, there would be nothing untoward with this. Boys will be boys. The reality is much the same in the West Bank. Fathers may look on in pride as their sons put on black and white *keffiyeh* and pretend to be fighting for the Palestinians but the reality is that most parents, as in most countries, wish their children to do well at school and find a job, and perhaps even attend university and become doctors or lawyers. They do not wish them to become involved in violent action. The priority of most young Palestinians is to find a job and establish and support a family. However, Israel's actions in the West Bank are depriving a new generation of Palestinians of these opportunities. With high unemployment and birth rates, the future for most looks bleak.

With many fathers out of work, increasingly families are struggling to afford university fees, a situation which commonly results in sons' education being given priority over daughters'. At university the difficulties of checkpoints and student arrests, and the general climate of occupation, make normal student life impossible. In the 1990s, 20% of students at Birzeit University came from Gaza. However, Israel now prevents Palestinians from Gaza from attending West Bank universities. Fewer students now attend Birzeit from the northern towns of Jenin and Tulkarm because of the difficulties in passing checkpoints. Israel also tries to isolate Palestinian universities by restricting contact with

Boys on a rainy day in Qalqilya.
Qalqilya is a major Palestinian city
located on the Green Line. Israel
has almost completely surrounded
the city with the Wall, separating
its inhabitants from their lands,
limiting their access to other
Palestinian towns, and
consequently depriving them
of their livelihoods.

universities in other countries. For example, it increasingly refuses permits for foreign tutors who wish to teach at Palestinian universities.

One female student told me that her university was split half and half between those who were interested in politics and wanted to change things and those who blocked the situation out of their minds and tried to pretend things were normal. Being involved in a political party on campus, particularly Hamas, is enough grounds for the Israelis to imprison a student. Birzeit University has at least 100 students imprisoned at any one time. Many are detained under administrative detention (where no charges need to be brought) for periods between 3 and 6 months. It is not therefore surprising that some just try to get on with their lives but is such behaviour also an acceptance of defeat?

Palestinians all over the West Bank have been worn down by the cumulative effects of occupation. They desperately want to be left alone in peace but the pressure applied on them by Israel is unrelenting. The Israeli government applies pressure on universities because it perceives that educated Palestinians pose a threat to Israel (which in reality they do not) and to its control of the West Bank (which clearly they do). Graduates can potentially organize, lead and inspire their people and they can communicate more effectively with the outside world. They can build businesses, revitalizing the economy, and build the infrastructure of a state. This prospect is abhorrent to Israel's establishment. By creating an atmosphere that restricts the flow of ideas and spirit of creativity on campus, and restricting movement between the Palestinian enclaves it has created, Israel hopes to weaken Palestinian resolve and identity.

There is a catch 22 for Israel here though. By restricting Palestinians' access to education, it makes them less attractive to other countries and means that fewer will be able to emigrate, therefore working against the Quiet Transfer, Israel's policy of "encouraging" Palestinian migration. Also, although it may be the case that Israel's repressive regime succeeds in producing a quiescent population prepared to accept subjugation as normal, with modern communications and media Palestinians will always have access to the outside world and be able to contrast it with their own. They will always be aware that they are a subject population deprived of true liberty and justice. As increasing numbers of children reach adulthood harbouring the angst of a traumatizing and deprived childhood, and facing a life of unemployment, the powder keg may explode again. More worrying still, with Palestinians turning increasingly to religion for solace, the door is open for the ideology of radical Islam to bring its influence to bear on an angry and impressionable youth.

Children playing with their new presents – plastic guns – on Eid Al-Adha, Qalandia refugee camp

"We try to encourage young people by teaching, not theoretically because they get fed up with that, but by doing. For example, we brought some kids from a Bethlehem refugee camp aged 10 to 13 years to our land and got them to speak about wishes for the future. One wanted to be a doctor, one an engineer. One girl about 10 years old said she wanted to die and started to cry. Her father was shot dead when very young and she never had the chance to know him so she hoped to meet him in heaven. The problem with our children is that we don't allow them to bring their frustration out. We gave her a camera to take some pictures of animals and nature, and told her to talk about it and she was encouraged by this. The message is that we are all important, even if we are not educated. We can all play a role in society and share our experiences with others."

Daoud, Bethlehem

Author's note

Daoud and his family have set up an organization called Tent of Nations which aims to bring people from different cultures, religions and backgrounds together to build bridges of understanding, reconciliation and peace. It also encourages international volunteers to show solidarity with Palestinians.

"I fear for the future of our children. They have no space to grow. The sea is fifteen miles away but they have never seen it.

They are frightened at checkpoints; they worry their dolls might be taken away. Israeli cars drive straight through while we wait for hours. Our children ask why? What are we supposed to say?"

Samar, a nurse from Birzeit

Boy looking towards passing
vehicles belonging to Israeli
settlers. He is sitting in a stationary
Palestinian taxi queuing at an
Israeli checkpoint on the road
between Nablus and Ramallah.

"Children here grow up with shootings, bombs and killings – they don't get an opportunity to laugh. We want to bring fun back. To resist the Wall in a positive way."

Imad, Palestinian Circus School

Bruce, a volunteer from the UK
Circus Space, and Imad

"485 houses were demolished by the Israelis in the attack. It took three years for them to be rebuilt. Refugees suffer from social, financial and psychological problems especially women and children. Violence is directed against other refugees in the camp, not just Israelis. Children are violent because everything they see is related to violence – martyrs, helicopters, lost fathers. Most have lost one member of their family. When given a choice of game they choose tanks and guns. They draw weapons.

Most men were dependent on work on the other side of the Green Line [in Israel]. Most people now depend on aid organizations. 70% [in the camp] are unemployed. 40 persons became disabled due to the intifada. People believe Abu Mazen [PA President Mahmoud Abbas] is selling out the refugees."

Community leader speaking about the IDF's attack on Jenin refugee camp in April 2002, during which 56 Palestinians were killed

Boys in Ramallah looking at
the wreckage of Palestinian
cars destroyed by Israeli
bulldozers during an incursion
several hours earlier. Five
Palestinians were killed.

"Al-Quds [Jerusalem] University has the only medical school in Palestine – we have medicine, dentistry, pharmacy, public health, medical professions, and other non-medical subject faculties.

Professors frequently spend two to three hours at Container checkpoint getting from their homes in Bethlehem so they miss lectures. The Israelis try to prevent foreign tutors from working here. We had some professors from France as volunteers. They worked for six to nine months and left for a holiday. When they came back, they were denied entry. Even Palestinian professors with US passports are denied entry – we have just had an economics professor refused at the airport. Meanwhile Israelis give permits to Chinese labourers to work on Israeli building sites.

The university has cooperation projects with Israeli universities but we have had to hold workshops in Turkey so we can meet.

In every university round the world there is life in the evening. Here it is dead after 4 p.m. because people think of roadblocks and getting back to their families.

The Israelis try to disturb our activities. If we plan a workshop and something happens, everything is disrupted. Sometimes there are checkpoints at the university gates. Last month we had a conference on refugees. We prepared for it for a year. Early in the morning we found a checkpoint at the entrance. They interrogated people as they arrived, including professors from the US, Canada and Egypt.

One day three years ago, the IDF blockaded the university with 5,000 students inside. I said to them, "Go away otherwise a stone will be thrown and we will have a massacre", but in the end we were all obliged to show our IDs to get out – they were looking for three or four students."

Member of staff, Al-Quds University

Hassan, a student at Birzeit
University, after having passed
through three checkpoints and
taken four hours to travel a distance
that should take at most 45 minutes

Palestinian student taking a photograph from a bus carrying international visitors as it begins its descent into the Jordan Valley. Israel has established an illegal permit system which prevents most West Bank Palestinians from visiting the valley, which Israel intends to annex in order to establish the Jordan River as its new eastern border.

12 | The collapse of Christianity

From the early years of Islam in the 8th century to the *nakba,* the majority of Palestine's inhabitants were Muslim. However, until the 20th century there were also communities of Christians and Jews coexisting with the Muslim population. Islam teaches that Christians and Jews as "Peoples of the Book" should be respected. Jews were only ever present in relatively small numbers and, since the Crusades, Christianity presented no real threat to Muslim rule. It was common to see Muslims, Christians and Jews worshipping at the same religious sites.

The colonization of Palestine by large numbers of Jews, the creation of Israel and Israel's annexation and occupation of Palestinian land, however, unleashed forces which have worked to separate the practitioners of these religions, a process which is still continuing. These forces were and are political in nature but they have worked to erode the peaceful coexistence of the past.

The conflict between Palestinian Muslims and Christians, and Israeli Jews was a consequence of mass Jewish immigration and colonization, and the forced flight of most of the Palestinian people. The same forces have, however, given rise to a new wave of emigration which is also doing great damage to religious plurality. Christians comprise approximately 10% of the Palestinian population worldwide but emigration has left the Christian population of the West Bank at between 1 and 2%. Christian Palestinians find it much easier to emigrate to the West than Muslims. Their religion and culture mean they can adapt much more easily to Western society. In the context of the pressure Israel imposes on Palestinian life, it is therefore not surprising that many Christians are choosing to leave.

One Christian said to me, "I can't see there being no Christians in Bethlehem in 10 years' time." Of course there will be, but how many? History does not encourage optimism. Many Christian villages in the Middle East have been abandoned over the years as depopulation has made them unsustainable. The imbalance between Muslims and Christians is changing the nature of Palestinian society. The number of Christians has perhaps fallen beneath the critical mass necessary for it to influence society. For example, Muslim women are increasingly adopting the hejab and this makes some Christian women uncomfortable. It is not that the hejab is a sign of submission. Indeed, Muslim Palestinian women stress that it gives no indication as to a woman's status or education. Rather, it is a fact that people generally feel more comfortable conforming, and as a community diminishes in size there are less of their own kind to identify with. Inevitably they feel more isolated, irrespective of the reasons for their marginalization. The Christian population in the West Bank is now such a small minority that a dynamic has been created whereby the

emigration of one Christian encourages his neighbour to leave. Also, it is largely the younger population which is emigrating, leaving the older, unproductive generations behind.

The problems of Christians in Palestine are sometimes portrayed in the western media as a result of Muslim imtimidation. This is untrue and Christian Palestinians make it clear that it is Israel's policies and, at the present time, particularly the Wall which are forcing them to leave. Traditionally, a higher proportion of Christians than Muslims have worked in the fields of trade and commerce and in many cases their livelihoods have been destroyed. The Wall is strangling towns all down the western boundary of the West Bank and Bethlehem is no exception. Bethlehem is predominantly a Muslim town but historically it has been a centre of Christian life in the West Bank. It was, however, always very closely linked with Jerusalem, the Old City being only 6 miles away. The two cities' inhabitants traded, worshipped and socialized together. Israel's separation of them by the Wall has brought Bethlehem to its knees. Most of its inhabitants once earned their living through tourism, working in hotels, transportation, carving ornaments from olive wood and such like. Now very few tourists come to Bethlehem and those that do are usually bussed in from Jerusalem for a brief visit before being whisked away again to spend their money in Israel. "Give me a chance and I'll leave the city and won't come back. I have a young son – it's impossible here", one shop owner said to me.

Palestinian Christians are particularly angry at the lack of support from Christians outside Palestine. They see Jews and Muslims around the world agitating on behalf of their faiths' interests in Palestine and particularly Jerusalem but they see no pressure being applied by Christian interests. One Christian said to me:

"Christians are a soft egg between two rocks. Why aren't the Christians asking for Jerusalem to be an international city? The Muslims are claiming it for themselves, so are the Jews. World Christians are not standing up. We are on the frontline and they do nothing. They could control the Jews and the Muslims if they wanted. The Churches are too busy fighting amongst themselves. The Orthodox are thieves – too busy renting property, the Catholics are assholes. I was raised as an Orthodox but I say I am a Christian. We are all Christians. Am I crazy today or am I right? You answer me that question – why don't the Christians stand up for us?"

This migration is a tragedy for the Palestinians and the world. The Christian community is an invaluable means of communication with the wider Christian world, particularly the US and Europe. The Palestinians have failed to take full advantage of this opportunity in the past. However, with the world increasingly polarized between western, quasi-Christian society and Muslim society, Christian Palestinians offer their people an opportunity to bridge the gap and deliver the message that their subjugation is a political and not religious issue.

Young man in the Christian
town of Taybeh

"This was the main road to Bethlehem, the richest one. Now there is a gate blocking the way to Bethlehem which the Israelis only open at Christmas and Easter for the Patriarch's procession. This is what I ask. As a Christian, we should be safe where Jesus was born. We should be able to pray in the Church of the Holy Sepulchre [in East Jerusalem]. It's the Holy Land. Bethlehem is like a big prison. We can't go to Ramallah or Jericho without permits which take a month to obtain, if they are granted. We used to take our children to Jerusalem where there are nice parks. Now all we can do is drive around Bethlehem.

I have four children. My brother-in-law has five children. We have fourteen people altogether in this apartment. We can't afford to heat it. Last winter our bones were hurting because it was so cold. My children were crying because of that. My son has contracted a serious and expensive foot infection from walking on contaminated land while sewage pipes were being rerouted because of the Wall. My husband has heart problems because of stress.

We are powerless. We don't want to hurt anybody. We want to feed our children. We want to live in peace. This is our aim in life. With Rachel's Tomb on one side and an army camp on the other we will have ten-metre walls on three sides of our building. We will be surrounded like a tomb. They are going to bury us alive with our nine children. We don't know what to do. Nobody gives us any help. No one cares, no one cares. How are we going to live? I am not political. I am not blaming anybody – the Israelis or the Palestinian Authority. I don't want a black mark against me. If that happens I won't be able to get permits to travel to Jerusalem. My second brother-in-law has moved to Jordan because he couldn't stand it anymore. Our stores are locked up accumulating dust. We can't sell them because we would only get 1% of their past value. All our neighbours have left. We are dying now, but alive. **"**

Mary, Bethlehem

The main road from Jerusalem to Bethlehem, now closed and cut in two by the Wall. The Wall has been routed around Rachel's tomb without regard to Palestinian residents so Israelis can visit it without crossing into Palestinian-controlled parts of Bethlehem.

"We are brothers in Bethlehem – Christian and Muslim. We live together, we suffer together, we are happy together. When the Israelis come to town they don't care – they shoot anybody. A Christian child, Johnny Talgiyeh, was shot in front of the church here – also Daniel. We are the same. We have a high level of cooperation between us.

Many people are leaving Bethlehem because of the Wall. There is no business, no European financial support, no tourists – we live in a big prison."

Adnan in his souvenir shop, Bethlehem

Adnan in his souvenir shop,
Bethlehem

"We run a private school but people struggle with the fees. There is 40% unemployment in Taybeh. Fifty-five people worked in a casino in Jericho. It closed because no Israelis or foreigners visit now. People also used to work in settlements. We try to find people work; we produce olive oil which we market in France in the fair trade sector.

Ramallah is 15 kilometres away but the Israelis closed the road because Ofra settlement is in between. Now we must use the back roads and the journey is 35 kilometres. With checkpoints it can take one or two hours.

The main problem is that people can't go to Jerusalem without a permit – a violation against freedom of religion. The Vatican Agreement of 1994 with Israel says Israel must give Christians free access to Jerusalem but even me, a priest, isn't allowed to go to Jerusalem freely. I need special permission. This may take weeks so I boycott it and try to get through anyway. I am protected as a priest. Others are jailed for six months at least for trying to cross into Jerusalem. Everything puts pressure on people to leave. The young are emigrating, the old remain. They can lose the right of return if they are away for more than three years. We have had to build care homes because the only old people's homes are in Jerusalem, which we cannot access because of the Wall.

I am against all forms of violence but you must understand that Palestinian violence is a consequence of a bigger violence, which is the occupation. Resistance is legal under international law but I believe it is better to use passive and non-violent means like Gandhi. "Olive branch resistance" is more powerful but nobody is hearing. We are prophets and voices in the wilderness."

Father Raed, Catholic priest, Taybeh

Father Raed, Catholic priest,
Taybeh

The Catholic Patriarch passes through a series of checkpoints surrounding Rachel's tomb, and which form part of the Wall, on his way from Jerusalem to Bethlehem on Christmas Eve. This road used to be the main road between Jerusalem and Bethlehem but, with the exception of the Christmas and Easter processions, Israel has closed it to vehicular traffic.

PART 3:

THE END GAME

13 | Israel's great gamble

Since its occupation of the West Bank in 1967, Israel's policies in the territory have worked towards the annexing of a minimum of 40% of West Bank land while keeping as much control over the remainder as possible. In conventional military terms, the West Bank is of strategic importance to Israel as at its most westerly point it is only 10 miles from the Israeli coast, potentially offering a hostile army based there an opportunity to cut Israel in two. In reality, Israel's nuclear capacity and its superior armed forces negate this threat. Israeli interests would be better served by reaching a lasting peace settlement with the Palestinians. However, the West is implicitly giving Israel its support for its implementation of a unilateral solution aimed at perpetuating its domination of the Palestinians.

The Oslo Accords gave Israel the pretext for implementing this solution. Israel has moved quickly under the cover of events in Gaza and the Iraq War to reconfigure the West Bank. By building the Wall, Israel has effectively annexed the Palestinian land which lies between it and the Green Line. By including the large settlement of Ariel behind the Wall it has secured access to the West Bank's main aquifer and it has divided the West Bank into three geographical units. Israel has successfully sub-divided these units into multiple Palestinian enclaves. The networks of Israeli roads, military installations and settlements that occupy the corridors and blocks of land allow Israel to operate its apartheid system of colonization. This infrastructure will allow Israel to lock down areas of the West Bank at will in the future. It also serves to weaken Palestinian identity and leave Palestinians in a state of hardship, thereby promoting emigration.

Given its success in achieving its objectives, it is unlikely that Israel will allow the enclaves to be reunited More likely, they will be linked by tunnels and fenced roads, thereby allowing Israel, the US and their European accomplices to claim that the basis for a viable Palestinian state has been created. However, these access corridors will continue to be subject to Israeli checkpoints and closures by which Israel will retain control. Although the US and Europe are likely to put enormous pressure on the Palestinian leadership to accept this "solution", it is unlikely that a Palestinian leader could agree to it. However, it may prove to be a *fait accompli.*

In the long term, however, Israel's success in implementing its unilateral solution depends on two things: the acceptance of the international community that the resultant Palestinian entity is sufficiently independent for justification of the status quo; and the prevention of significant Palestinian violence against Israel and its citizens.

Given that the international community shows no appetite for criticizing, let alone imposing sanctions on, Israel, it is difficult to conceive of a situation whereby Israel would

These photos were taken within 500 metres of each other. They meet at a checkpoint on the horizon of each picture.

Commuters leaving Ma'ale Adumim settlement, 2 November 2005

Road leading to the Palestinian town of Azarya, two minutes walk from the entrance to Ma'ale Adumim settlement, 1 November 2005

be obliged to address the inequalities faced by Palestinians in the West Bank. However, the US's unqualified support for Israel may ultimately do Israel no favours. Like a child left alone in a sweet shop, Israel cannot resist the temptation to take more and more Palestinian land. Consequently, there is a danger that at some point along the line Israel's status as a democratic country will be challenged and its apartheid regime exposed on the international stage. If by then Israel has so effectively incorporated the West Bank into Israel that a viable Palestinian state is impossible, it will be faced with the doomsday scenario of enfranchising West Bank Palestinians and transforming Israel from a Jewish to a secular state if it wishes to regain its status as a democracy.

More pertinently, Israel must continue to restrict Palestinian violence. The purpose of the Wall was primarily demographic – to create the fiction of a two-state scenario. It was also, as we have seen, a land grab. Israel, however, sold the Wall to its people and the world on the basis of security, its *raison d'etre* for continuing the occupation and for most actions associated with it. Certainly separation of the majority of West Bank Palestinians from Israelis by the Wall and other security measures has reduced the opportunity for spontaneous and poorly planned attacks. However, will it completely remove the possibility of suicide attacks within Israel? Israel has separated itself from 2 million Palestinians in the West Bank but it has left almost 300,000 West Bank Palestinians on the Jerusalem side of the Wall. As the forces of separation bite on them, hitherto quiescent East Jerusalem Palestinians may become radicalized and present a threat from within.

Successive Israeli governments have promoted the idea, amongst its people and internationally, that the Arab nations wish to see Israel swept into the sea and that Israel is constantly under threat. This is clearly not the case given Israel's military strength and the secure peace treaties with Jordan and Egypt. However, it is widely believed, both inside and outside Israel. A moderate, immigrant Israeli of European birth said to me:

"Israeli politics is governed by Realpolitik. If you don't send soldiers into the Old City for two weeks they will think we have given up and start a new *intifada*. If we give them a little, they will want more until we are driven out. We have to make sure they are sure in their minds that we are more powerful."

The separation of the peoples by the Wall will only serve to increase the gap of understanding between them, making it far more difficult for them to reach an accommodation. For the moment, the reduction in Palestinian attacks in Israel due to the Wall and Hamas' commitment to politics, and the reduced profile of peace blocs within Israeli society, have given Israeli Jews a more comfortable and insulated life. The status quo no longer seems so bad for them. However, if they find that a new generation of desperate Palestinians succeeds in mounting a terror campaign within Israel, they may find it even more difficult to make peace.

These photos were taken within two kilometres of each other.

Palestinian sheep grazing on land in the valley beneath Ma'ale Adumim settlement, 1 November 2005

Green space in Ma'ale Adumim settlement, 1 November 2005

The eastern section of Ma'ale Adumim settlement viewed from the western section with the Judean desert, an Israeli closed military area, in the background. The Wall is being built deep into the West Bank to include Ma'ale Adumim on the Jerusalem side. It will therefore cut off the southern West Bank (including Bethlehem and Hebron) from the rest of the West Bank.

"Do I have any hope?
Not in my lifetime.
I am 35."

Ihrahim, refugee

The Palestinians are running out of options. They never had many open to them in the first place but with the West's rejection of their democratically elected government, all avenues seem to have closed. The Oslo Accords ushered in a Palestinian government which, if not an instrument of Israel, was happy to perpetuate the status quo while its members lived relatively privileged, comfortable lives. The Palestinian people may not have all recognized the extent of collusion between their government and Israel but they could see the corruption at its heart. Consequently, they elected Hamas, partly as a protest vote and partly because, at ground level, they could see that Hamas offered clean politicians and a structure that aided the disadvantaged.

With the rejection of Hamas by the US and Europe, despite the fact that Hamas's mandate was based on a 78% turnout (almost twice what one might expect in the US or the UK), Palestinians have recognized the fraud perpetrated on them by Israel and the West. The West continues to demand that Hamas recognizes Israel even though Israel has never accepted the principle of a viable Palestinian state. It demands Hamas gives up all violence (not simply suicide bombings against civilians) even though as an occupied people Palestinians have a legitimate right to resist, and Israel continues to use illegal and excessive force in targeting its leadership and Palestinians in general. It also demands that Palestinians respect prior agreements when it is Israel that has consistently breached them.

Some Palestinians would perhaps accept any settlement, so desperate are they for peace, if they could be certain of its implementation and permanence. However, they know that peace on Israel's terms is likely to be illusory. In any case the majority have drawn a line in the sand and are not prepared to compromise on what is rightfully theirs – a state within the internationally accepted 1967 border, with its capital in Jerusalem. Also, although few observers would agree, many Palestinians believe that time is on their side; that if they hold fast in East Jerusalem and retain their faith in God, the injustices perpetrated against them will be remedied.

Recently, Israel and the US have been engaged in a process to subvert democracy and return Fatah to power, with the ultimate goal of forcing the Palestinian Authority to accept the establishment of a Palestinian "state" on Israel's terms. Rather than serving its time in opposition and reforming itself, Fatah has participated in this process, accepting US-funded weapons and promoting armed conflict with Hamas. By pursuing this policy, Mahmoud Abbas, the Palestinian President and leader of Fatah, risked a civil war which would have been calamitous for the Palestinian people. It seems, however, that he has

Opposite
Al-Aqsa Martyrs Brigade
martyr poster, Tulkarm

pulled back and committed to a unity government brokered by Saudi Arabia. By joining with Fatah it could be argued that Hamas has compromised its principles and betrayed the trust of those Palestinians who voted to expel the existing corrupt regime. On the other hand, Mahmoud Abbas and Fatah may give enough legitimacy to the Palestinian government to enable relations with the EU and ultimately the US to be restored, thereby bringing an end to the suspension of aid. Meanwhile Hamas may be able to provide the steel to strengthen Mahmoud Abbas's negotiating position with the West and to some extent restore his people's confidence in him.

Unfortunately though, there is nobody in Palestinian politics who seems capable of uniting all Palestinians. For all his faults, Arafat was loved by the people because he was a great orator who spoke to the people as one of them. In contrast, Mahmoud Abbas lacks that charisma and has been emasculated on the international stage by Israel and the US. There are younger Palestinians with the energy and determination to change things for the better, even within Fatah. The PA has survived Ariel Sharon's onslaught and its institutions, created by conscientious governmental staff, have proved surprisingly robust. However, Palestinian society is built around a respect for its elders and this, combined with the existing powerbases within Fatah, perpetuates the status quo. A student, Farah, said to me, "Which way will society go? Violence or resignation? You can never guess, the human being is a really weird thing and you never know when a person will give up hope. I know lots of people who could be good leaders but they will never be because they are not part of the system." Even if a leader emerged who might be capable of uniting the Palestinian people, it is difficult to see how he or she could mobilize support without Israeli intervention.

Palestinians have therefore engaged in an essentially non-violent *intifada*, a violent *intifada* and democratic elections while being lured into one empty peace process after another. Meanwhile, Israel is turning the West Bank into a big prison on the Gazan model. If the unity government fails to deliver, where can they turn? The obvious answer is to God. Palestinians, both Muslim and Christian, are increasingly turning to their religions to find solace. This is not out of indoctrination but because they can see that nationalist politics is not working for them. As one Palestinian put it, "The nation is collectively realizing that they have no power and their only option is surrender. The only way of avoiding defeat is to look to God and move towards radical religion." It is therefore inevitable as the prison doors close around the Palestinians and what little hope they have in earthly power is extinguished, that new generations of Palestinians will be radicalized by their faiths.

Opposite

View through a broken window, Ramallah

"Palestine has lost its dignity, it has been raped. Israel has destroyed our people's common values – in nationalism, in resistance, in democracy and in religion.

My main fear is the brain drain which will kill our nation. The occupation drains the potential for creativity, literature, political thought and economics, and nobody seems to talk about this.

We are in dire need of a new Edward Said. We need to embrace openness of thought and start communicating effectively with the world. Of course this will not be an easy task, knowing how Israel influences world media, but we have to work on it because there is no other choice. We cannot resign ourselves to such facts because we owe it to ourselves and our legitimate cause.

Everybody is doing their own bit while the collective consciousness seems to be absent. NGOs are busy trying to get their financing, Fatah is not able to play a constructive opposition role and Hamas has been unable to understand the difference between the rights and responsibilities of a real government. What we are lacking is a comprehensive long-term vision based on a strong consensus of all the stakeholders in Palestinian society both inside the Territories and amongst the diaspora.

You must be strong as a politician and stick to your principles. You can't be afraid to lose your job. To make history you have to be history. Who is like this? No one. We need such a leader – a new Messiah – someone daring, not afraid of telling the truth, someone who would be prepared to sacrifice his life for the sake of his people. I wish I could do it."

Lily Habash, Senior Palestinian Governance Expert

Lily Habash, Senior Palestinian
Governance Expert

"A problem with Arab society is we respect our elders too much. The older generation are waiting for a Messiah, waiting for the superpowers to do something and they don't realize that for us to succeed we must develop a movement of the people. We all have to share in it: children, young people and women, using our own capacities. Peace must grow like a tree from the bottom up. It cannot be imposed from above – just look at Iraq. I used to have many friends who were active and motivated but they have now left the country because they see that there is no hope and future for this country and have been blocked by the difficult political and economic situation.

There is nobody in Palestinian political society now who could unite Palestinians. The Arab mentality divides into tribes and families and religion so it is very difficult to unite people. What can unite people is changes on the ground – not unfulfilled programs and promises but achievements. As Palestinians we shouldn't always play the victim role. We must be motivated to change the situation. We must ask ourselves "What can I do, what can I change?" We must change our image in the world. Why invest in buying guns from Israel; we should invest in media. When our politicians go abroad they should forget meeting politicians and motivate the Palestinian expat community. Expats can invest in hospitals and economic projects. This can help all Palestinians, inside and outside Palestine, to play a role in building up their country and shape their future in their own hands. Let's show people we want to learn, be creative and develop new ideas like solar power. Let's play sport abroad and fly the Palestinian flag. We must disprove the Israeli story."

Daoud, Bethlehem

Teacher and class, Al-Khass near Bethlehem. Al-Khass has been separated from its neigbouring village, Al-Nouman, by the Wall.

Mural on wall in
Deheisheh refugee camp,
Bethlehem

15 | It doesn't have to be this way

When one sees the desperate situation of the Palestinians in the West Bank, it is difficult not to be angry with the world. Indeed one marvels at their friendliness and hospitality given their treatment by the international community over the last 100 years. One Palestinian student said to me: "They try to steal our lives, to delete our ID, our personality. They take our land and treat us like animals… but please show we enjoy life." If there is enjoyment, however, it is born out the necessity to live in the moment because there are no guarantees of what tomorrow will bring. What Palestinians do have is a solidarity – a commitment to family and friendships – which sustains them in their helplessness.

It was not inevitable that things would be this way. Israel has had opportunities to break the cycle of dispossession and exile, and reach an accommodation with the Palestinian people. Its leaders could have chosen to abide by UN Resolution 242 and withdraw from the West Bank in 1967. They could have followed through with their commitment to negotiate a settlement made in the Camp David Accords in 1978. They could have chosen to build on the Oslo Accords of 1993 and 1995 by moving to a two state solution. They could have welcomed the Arab League's promise of recognition of the state of Israel made in 2002. However, in each case the Israeli establishment has spurned the opportunity for peace and retreated into its colonial, expansionist mindset, increasing settlement building and strengthening its hold over the West Bank and its people. Dominated by the military, the most stable institution in Israeli society, constrained by the history of political Zionism, and free from effective international sanction, Israeli governments of all complexions have allowed the machinery of dispossession and occupation to roll on.

In recent years the "peace process" has been reduced to a negotiation between Ariel Sharon and the US. Mahmoud Abbas, the Palestinian President, has been ignored. Now with Sharon's departure from the political scene, his deputy Ehud Olmert, is continuing his policies. What seems certain is that, for the foreseeable future, the US will always side with Israel against its own foreign policy interests. A strong US President could bring Israel to heel. Withdrawing the massive amounts of aid which the US gives to Israel would have a very damaging effect on Israel's economy and depriving Israel of military support would have an enormous psychological effect. In such a situation, the rest of the world would in all likelihood support the US approach. The US's commitment to Israel, however, was strengthened in the aftermath of 9/11 as Israel suceeded in portraying itself as a key partner in the "War against Terror". In fact, US foreign policy in the Middle East in the twenty-first century has been so closely aligned to that of Israel that it has essentially

Bakers, Old City, Nablus

become an arm of the Israeli government. The black and white, "with us or against us" approach to US foreign policy combined with the strong influence of the Jewish and evangelical Christian lobbies and George Bush's neo-conservative aides has isolated the Palestinians.

Meanwhile, the Europeans, Russians and even the UN seem content to acquiesce. Palestinian pressure groups have little influence compared to the Jewish lobby. Some world leaders may believe that Israel could be persuaded to withdraw behind the Wall and that a settlement could be reached on such a basis. If so, they must have the unrealistic expectation that the US will exert sufficient pressure on Israel to enforce a settlement, and a lack of comprehension of the importance of Jerusalem to the Palestinians.

The extent of Israeli infrastructure and population in the West Bank makes the creation of a viable Palestinian state in the future unlikely and some Palestinians recognize this. One said to me, "This is part of Israel – it is a fact on the ground. The solution is to give us freedom – let us live like neighbours side by side." And there lies the answer: peace comes with equality, justice and freedom. The Palestinians of the Occupied Territories therefore face at best marginalization at the limits of the Israeli state under the rule of a Palestinian Authority dependant more on Israel for its power than its own electorate. The Palestinian Authority is little more than an administrative body. To date it has not been capable of true political leadership. Now that the Hamas government has been rejected by the West, many Palestinians doubt the legislative assembly's value.

A single democratic state in Palestine is not possible while Israel remains a state for the benefit of one ethnic group. Judaism is embedded within Israel's laws. This would perhaps be acceptable within the context of an exclusively Jewish state. However, over one million Christian and Muslim Palestinians living in Israel, descended from those who remained within Israel's borders at the time of the 1948 armistice, have Israeli citizenship. While Jews of increasingly suspect lineage are welcome with open arms from all over the world to bolster the Jewish population, millions of Palestinian refugees on Israel's borders are denied a return to their homeland.

Israel is held up as a beacon of democracy in the Middle East by its supporters in the West while in fact it continues to act as a colonial power, depriving 4.5 million Palestinians of the right to freedom and justice in their own lands. For too long the western world has judged Israel by different rules dictated by Holocaust guilt and sympathy. As one Palestinian said to me, "What did we do to deserve this? It was not us who killed the Jews in World War II". It is shameful that a Jewish state which so fervently, and justifiably, fights to maintain public awareness of the horror of the Holocaust and anti-semitism, should itself at the same time oppress another race. Apologists for Israel talk of moral relativism and justify the West's failure to live up to its own ideals by reference to even worse

Palestinian boys, Hebron

breaches committed by its enemies. However, if we accept this philosophy, we will be dragged down to their level. Indeed, we are seeing it happen around us as our governments, in the name of security, strip away basic human rights hard fought for over the centuries. Israel, with its militarized state, walls and ruthlessness may be successful in minimizing the future Palestinian threat. However, liberal western society is much more open to attack from Islamists, many of whom draw motivation from the Palestinians' plight

The great tragedy for the world is that a resolution of the conflict would deprive Al-Qaeda and its offshoots of one of their main sources of support within the Islamic world. However, the West's failure to accept that Arab politics, like its culture, is naturally influenced by the region's Islamic tradition and to trust the vast majority of peace loving, moderate Arabs to develop genuine democratic institutions within this tradition, only serves to strengthen the forces of radical Islam. Faced with these differences, the instinctive reaction of the US is to see "westernized" Israel as a bastion in the Middle East. However, Israel with its estimated 400 nuclear warheads and fourth largest army in the world no longer needs defending at all costs. In reality, western interests would be better served by reaching an accommodation with the Palestinians which would allow them to establish a genuinely viable, democratic state which can stand as an example and inspiration to the other peoples of the Middle East.

Meanwhile, Israel's expansionist, militarized establishment continually works to unite its people behind a fear and loathing of Palestinians. Some may fear peace and what future it might bring. However, opinion polls consistently show a majority in favour of a peace settlement. In 2003, former Israeli and Palestinian negotiators agreed the Geneva Accord which set out a final settlement based on a viable Palestinian state with Jerusalem as a dual capital. Although not sanctioned by either party, it demonstrated that peace is not impossible. Israel was created by the actions of the Zionist movement and the western powers, and looks to biblical history for its birthright. However, only the Palestinians can give Israel true legitimacy in the eyes of other Middle Eastern peoples and governments. Palestinians want peace. They want equality. They want a home. Mohammed, Shadi and Ibrahim are not exceptions but the rule. For most the desire for a state comes not from a nationalist fervour but an acceptance that only by ruling themselves will they achieve freedom and equality. At some point, if Israel is to continue to be seen as a modern, democratic country, it must come to terms with the existence of the Palestinian people and their rights as human beings. In the words of Edward Said:

"Palestine/Israel... is the place where two peoples, whether they like it or not, live inextricably linked lives, tied together by history, war, daily contact, and suffering. ... There is no substitute for seeing these two communities as equal to each other in rights and expectations, and then proceeding from there to do justice to their living actualities."

Palestinians walking beside a
country road

"We want peace. Not just us Christians. Not just our town. All of Palestine.

We have our culture. We have our customs. We have our language and [land] certificates. The Jews arrive and learn their language on arrival. They are given the double promise by the Zionist movement. They can have a car and a house in the US and Israel so they say why not? We haven't been able to go to Jerusalem for four years.

As for the settlement, did they take it by paper? No they took it by force. We were told to stay inside for three days and in that time they built it.

We know our rights, we know our history, but we have no power. Where are the human rights?

We know that people think differently from their governments in Europe. But they are democracies, they can change their governments."

Farah, Taybeh

Palestinian wedding procession,
Ramallah

"The problem between the Jews and the Palestinians is Jerusalem and the occupation. If the Jews go back to the 1967 borders, I tell you every Palestinian will go looking for an Israeli friend. There will be nothing between them but peace. But Jews believe that if they return to those borders, the Palestinians will demand more."

Abd Muin Sadaqa, High Priest of the Samaritans,
a biblical religious community split between the West Bank and
Israel who maintain a line of strict impartiality

Abd Muin Sadaqa,
High Priest of the Samaritans

Skateboards and toffee apples,
Nablus

Bibliography

In preparing this book I read the following books and articles:

Carter, Jimmy, *Palestine: Peace Not Apartheid* (New York: Simon & Schuster, 2006)

Cook, Jonathan, *Blood and Religion: The Unmasking of the Jewish State* (London: Pluto Press, 2006)

Dolphin, Ray, *The West Bank Wall: Unmaking Palestine* (London: Pluto Press, 2006)

Findley, Paul, *They Dare to Speak Out: People and Institutions Confront Israel's Lobby* (Chicago: Lawrence Hill Books, 2003)

Finkelstein, Norman, *Image and Reality of the Israel-Palestine Conflict* (London: Verso, 2003)

Hroub, Khaled, *Hamas: A Beginner's Guide* (London: Pluto Press, 2006)

Kretzmer, David, *The Occupation of Justice: The Supreme Court of Israel and the Occupied Territories* (New York: The State University of New York Press, 2002)

Mansfield, Peter, *A History of the Middle East* (London: Penguin, 2003)

Mearsheimer, John and Walt, Stephen, *The Israel Lobby* (London Review of Books Vol. 28 no. 6 dated 23 March 2006)

Neumann, Michael, *The Case Against Israel* (Edinburgh: Counterpunch, 2005)

Pappe, Ilan, *The Ethnic Cleansing of Palestine* (Oxford: Oneworld, 2006)

Reinhart, Tanya, *Israel/Palestine: How to End the War of 1948* (New York: Seven Stories Press, 2002)

Reinhart, Tanya, *The Road Map to Nowhere: Israel/Palestine since 2003* (London: Verso, 2006)

Information sources

There are many non-governmental organizations recording data on the conflict and the conditions of Palestinians living in the Occupied Territories. Indeed it must be one of the most documented places on earth. It is a measure of Israel's success in controlling the media agenda that this information largely remains within the realm of those already aware of the situation.

In researching this book I have largely restricted myself to use of data from organizations widely respected for their impartiality, namely:

Amnesty International, www.amnesty.org

B'Tselem (The Israeli Information Center for Human Rights in the Occupied Territories), www.btselem.org

OCHA (UN Office for the Coordination of Humanitarian Affairs), www.ochaonline.un.org

There are, however, many other such organizations doing valuable work which those wishing to learn more about the situation may consult. They include:

Al Haq, www.alhaq.org

The Applied Research Institute – Jerusalem, www.arij.org

Conflicts Forum, www.conflictsforum.org

The Foundation for Middle East Peace, www.fmep.org

Geneva Initiative, www.geneva-accord.org

HDIP (Health, Development, Information and Policy Institute), www.hdip.org

PASSIA (Palestinian Academic Society for the Study of International Affairs), www.passia.org

Activist organizations include:

BADIL, www.badil.org

The Israeli Committee against House Demolitions, www.icahd.org

The International Solidarity Movement, www.palsolidarity.org

The Palestinian Solidarity Campaign, www.palestinecampaign.org

Rabbis for Human Rights, www.rhr.israel.net

The Stop the Wall Coalition, www.stopthewall.org

Acknowledgements

This book would not have been possible without the openness and friendliness of Palestinians in the West Bank.

I would like to thank all the people who have helped me develop this project, particularly those Palestinians who have agreed to appear in this book. Thank you also to Akram, Esmat, Farah, Mohammed and Saleh for their valuable help in translating and helping to set up meetings, and to Dan, Emma, Juliette, Mark, Sam and Sarah for their help in reviewing.

Lastly, I would like to thank the students and staff of Birzeit University, near Ramallah, who offered me my first experience of the West Bank and who have helped me greatly since. Those wishing to contribute to the Palestinian cause might consider contributing to The Friends of Birzeit University, a British charity supporting education at the university (www.fobzu.org).